DATE DUE

The
Bleeding
Of America

This book is dedicated
to justice for all people,
individually and as nations.

Those who cannot remember the past are condemned to repeat it.
— George Santayana

The Bleeding Of America

By
HERMAN H. DINSMORE

Western ★ ★ Islands

First Printing, September 1974
Second Printing, December 1974
Third Printing, May 1975
Fourth Printing, September 1975
Second Edition, April 1976
Third Edition, October 1977

Third edition copyright 1977 by Herman H. Dinsmore.
Preface copyright 1977 by Western Islands
395 Concord Avenue
Belmont, Massachusetts 02178
Printed in the United States of America.

ISBN: 0-88279-126-5

Table of Contents

Acknowledgments

The author's debt to the many persons who, wittingly or unwittingly, contributed to the creation of this book is great, and he happily acknowledges his obligation to them. In cities and towns all across this nation, they have given him tips, books, pamphlets, and every encouragement to collect the materials for a book with a larger point of view than *All The News That Fits*.

The idea that the United States of America was under attack from some of its own citizens developed very slowly in the writer's mind. It was not until he read Dr. Medford Evans' *The Secret War for the A-Bomb* that he became convinced that a genuine effort was under way to establish a global check on this country — to balance other nations against it, to prevent it from winning wars; in short, to clip the wings of the American eagle.

The author would like to name *all* those who encouraged him, but the list would be too long. His gratitude is nonetheless extended to them for all the help they have given in the preparation of this book.

Preface to the Third Edition

HERMAN H. DINSMORE WORKED for the *New York Times* for thirty-four years, nine as editor of the International Edition. Out of that experience came a book entitled *All The News That Fits*, an exposé of the biases of the *Times*. In the last few years Mr. Dinsmore's understanding of the American crisis has deepened, and the title of this book indicates that change: The subject is no longer the most influential newspaper in the nation, but the nation itself.

In changing the focus of his writing, Mr. Dinsmore has set before us an example of intellectual growth. So many conservative writers are instances of arrested growth that it is refreshing to find someone like Herman Dinsmore who has the intellectual courage — and ability — to move from a detail (the bias of the communications media, for example) to a perception of the larger picture of what is happening to the American Republic.

This is not to belittle those writers who have profitably called our attention to the details, for without them there would be no larger picture to be seen. The greatest paintings display the greatest attention to detail. It is, rather, to reprove, if only mildly, those who have become so specialized in their concerns that they cannot — or will not — perceive the interconnections between their discoveries and the discoveries of others.

Perhaps *The Bleeding of America* would be a good starting place for those who suffer from the intellectual analogue of tunnel vision. In this short book, Herman Dinsmore steps back and takes a look at the larger picture, and in so doing shows us how some of the details fit together. Many of us, unfortunately, still believe that political events are not planned — they just happen. The more sophisticated among us may mumble something about the Forces of History, but generally we tend to believe that things, both great and small, just happen. After all, the universe is governed by chance — or so the scientists tell us — and that universe includes political affairs.

Consequently, people who buy milk Monday evening for Tuesday's breakfast continue to believe that assassinations, wars, and presidential nominations just happen. The idea that there may be someone or some organization planning those events is as remote from their minds as the details of Chinese history. Of course, we must not fall into the trap of saying that all political events are planned by any one group or individual. What we need to say is that the commanding events in political affairs are made by men who have a fairly well thought out plan about the kind of world they desire. George Orwell described that world as a boot stamping on a human face — forever.

It is our purpose in publishing this revised and updated edition of *The Bleeding of America* to prevent Orwell's vision from being realized by those who planned Pearl Harbor, the subjugation of Central Europe, and the Vietnamese War. Not believing that things just happen, Western Islands is committed to a publishing program designed to educate the American people in the history and virtues of the American Republic and the conspiracy that plans to destroy it. *The Bleeding of America* is the latest of our growing series of such books and we are pleased to commend it to all Americans.

Western Islands

CHAPTER 1

How To Construct
An Enemy

*In history nothing is more agreeable than simple
and lucid brevity.*

— Cicero

THERE IS NO BOOK known to this writer that explains the basic
philosophy underlying the deliberate transfer of power from the
United States to the Soviet Union and also provides the details of
this transfer, which began with President Franklin D. Roosevelt.
Following the outbreak of World War II, the United States
frenetically sent vast stocks of additional materials — atomic,
military, and industrial blueprints and diplomatic documents — to
the Russians, whose agents were being given a free run in our nation. Since that massive beginning, the transfer of power and
possessions, including bomb components from Los Alamos, has
continued consistently.

It is incorrect to call this *appeasement.* Prime Minister Neville
Chamberlain appeased the Nazis in 1938 because Britain was weak.
The United States has never been weak in relation to the Soviet
Union. On the contrary, the United States always has been the
stronger. Indeed, America saved the Russians from defeat in World
War II. (The authority for that statement is the best — Joseph
Stalin himself, who said at Teheran in 1943: "Without the United
States as a source of motors, this war would have been lost."* It
was moderate praise for American help that went far beyond
motors.)

America and Russia in a Changing World, by W. Averell Harriman, page 23.

1

The transfer of American power to the USSR has now become a fixed national policy supported by some to construct an enemy, and by others who hope vaguely to convert an enemy into a friend for trade and money-making purposes. These two prongs of United States Government policy, the effort to build an enemy and the desire to make money and gain a friend, suggest that either result would have been generally satisfactory. But since an enemy is what the United States got, it must be assumed that achievement of this goal was the *more* satisfactory of the two to the individuals who conceived United States foreign policy.[1]

That the great majority of the American people were unaware of what was happening is not open to doubt, for even the most knowledgeable among them have expressed great surprise and concern on hearing a presentation of the facts. On April 13, 1972, the writer spoke to the District of Columbia Chapter of the Military Order of the World Wars at the Army and Navy Club in Washington. He discussed the startling revelations contained in the book *The Secret War for the A-Bomb*, by Medford Evans — a brilliant and fearless statement of the probability that atomic bombs had been stolen from Los Alamos, Oak Ridge, and Hanford. (Dr. Evans was the security officer of the United States Atomic Energy Commission in the early 1950's, but resigned when his security recommendations were rejected.) His book, published in Chicago in 1953, was never reviewed by the newspapers in New York, Boston, or Washington. But two weeks after that talk, which may have been the first public expression (certainly in Washington) on the subject of atomic bomb thefts, a story in *The New York Times* offered some support for Dr. Evans' strong hypothesis. On April 26, 1972, the *Times* reported the opposition of thirty-one scientists and other professional persons to the Nixon Administration's plan to build a nuclear breeder reactor for the production of electricity. The protesters questioned whether such plants would be safe and asserted that some of the plutonium generated might be secretly "diverted" — that is, stolen — for the illegal manufacture of atomic bombs. Thus the *Times* recognized the possibility of such theft nineteen years after Dr. Evans' attempt to bring the matter before the public was smothered by the press.[2]

2

How To Construct An Enemy

Although this writer was an editor at the *Times* for some years (it was his duty as editor of the International Edition to know every story that went into the paper each day), as late as 1971 he knew nothing about *The Secret War for the A-Bomb* or its major thesis. He had heard nothing about the diaries of Major George Racey Jordan until 1969, seventeen years after their publication. (*From Major Jordan's Diaries* was reviewed in *The New York Times*, but very quietly, and in the Sunday Book Section. That book, which had considerable news value, deserved more prominent treatment.) Books written by scholars and professors show that their authors had a similar lack of knowledge of current events and recent history. The many volumes written by members of the Roosevelt, Truman, and succeeding Administrations, which make no mention of these events, fail deplorably to impart essential knowledge, whether because of their author's ignorance or through deliberate omissions.

For instance, at the Potsdam conference of President Truman, Prime Minister Attlee of Britain, and Premier Stalin, Mr. Truman told Stalin about the explosion of the first atomic bomb at Alamogordo, New Mexico, July 16, 1945. Mr. Truman wrote in his *Memoirs,* Vol. I, page 416:

> At Potsdam, as elsewhere, the secret of the atomic bomb was kept closely guarded. We did not extend the very small circle of Americans who knew about it. Churchill naturally knew about the atomic bomb project from its very beginning, because it had involved the pooling of British and American technical skill.
>
> On July 24 I casually mentioned to Stalin that we had a new weapon of unusual destructive force. The Russian Premier showed no special interest. All he said was that he was glad to hear it and hoped we would make "good use of it against the Japanese."

Secretary of State James F. Byrnes, who was present at that conference, commented in his book, *Speaking Frankly,** on Mr. Truman's colloquy with Stalin:

> Stalin's only reply was that he was glad to hear of the bomb

Speaking Frankly, by James F. Byrnes, page 263.

and he hoped we would use it. I was surprised at Stalin's lack of interest. I concluded that he had not grasped the importance of the discovery. I thought that the following day he would ask for more information about it. *He did not.* [Emphasis added.]

Seemingly, neither the President nor the Secretary of State knew that the United States had shipped enormous quantities of materials for making atomic bombs (nearly 23 million pounds by 1944) to the Soviet Union, and that the Manhattan Project and State Department were honeycombed with spies and agents of the Soviet Government, who were keeping Stalin fully informed on every development. Mr. Truman's statement strongly suggests that he did indeed feel that "the secret of the atomic bomb was kept closely guarded." But so far as the Russians were concerned, this was not the case, though the American people were totally in the dark about it. Mr. Byrnes's words indicate that he believed, since Stalin did not grasp the importance of the discovery, that the Soviet Premier did not know what was going on. Major Jordan wrote in his *Diaries* that Stalin probably knew more about the bomb than Truman and Byrnes together.

This is a remarkable instance of probable misinformation at the top. For we know that the Russians had been desperately eager to get every scrap of information and material regarding the atomic bomb since at least 1942, and that the U.S. Lend-Lease Administrator, Harry Hopkins, with strong support from President Roosevelt, had been just as eager to give all to the Russians.

Charles E. Bohlen, interpreter for President Truman at Potsdam, was present when Mr. Truman told Stalin through interpreter V. N. Pavlov about the bomb. Mr. Bohlen wrote in his book, *Witness to History,** that it seemed to him the President did not say to Stalin that the weapon exploded was an atomic bomb, and in any case, the Soviet Premier showed no great interest. Bohlen said he looked intently at Stalin's face as the President spoke, and it was so unresponsive that a question arose in Bohlen's mind as to whether Stalin had grasped the significance of what the President was saying. But in fact, some years later Marshal Georgi

Witness to History, by Charles E. Bohlen, page 237.

K. Zhukov disclosed in his memoirs that Stalin on that same night had ordered a message sent to the Russian scientists who were also working to build an atomic bomb, instructing them to speed up their efforts.

Mr. Bohlen was one of the most astute American diplomats ever sent to the Soviet Union. His book has become a guidepost for his fellow citizens, though he knew relatively little about the enormous build-up of the Soviet Union for the purpose of establishing a balance of power against the country for which he worked so long and so well.

It is entirely possible that Mr. Truman, while serving as Vice President to Franklin Roosevelt, and Mr. Byrnes, then Secretary of State, were not informed about the vast shipments of atomic information and materials to the Russians. General Leslie R. Groves, commander of the Manhattan Project that constructed the atomic bomb, was not informed of those shipments until they were brought to his attention by Major Jordan in 1949. (And President Roosevelt, of course, had done little to train Mr. Truman for the Presidency.) We still do not know the whole story, because many of the documents — those that were not sent to Russia — are classified. Indeed, that part of the atomic bomb story is still a "closely guarded" secret, at least in the United States.

Those of us who, in our adult years, lived through the various phases in the reduction of U.S. power vis-à-vis the Soviet Union did so in stunned disbelief at what was being allowed to happen to the strongest nation on earth. Unfortunately, most citizens, like this writer, had no real grasp of what was going on. The pitfalls of current history are many. When a deliberate effort is made to confuse and mislead the public, the resulting chaos can provide a cover for strange behavior on the part of the communications media, with regard to domestic as well as foreign affairs. Those victimized by the media may not know for years what hit them, though now, gradually, the truth is becoming known.[3]

The steps followed in creating a balance of power against the

United States by building Soviet Russia into an enemy complete with atomic bombs were as follows:

1. Make the USSR an atomic power by supplying millions of pounds of bomb-making materials during World War II and afterward, probably providing the component parts of the bombs themselves.

2. Build up the Soviet Union industrially to help make it the equal of the United States. This was being done even while the USSR was fighting the U.S. in Korea and Vietnam, expanding into Cuba, and gaining other footholds in Asian, African, and Western Hemisphere countries such as Chile (which now has been regained for freedom).

3. Permit the Soviet Government to take over Eastern Europe, including Poland, the very country in which the Second World War was ignited.[4]

4. Hand China over to the Communists.

5. Encourage "national liberation" movements everywhere.

6. Fight no-win wars as part of a policy of "containment."

7. Permit the Communists to organize and control the United Nations, and then to use this incipient world government to expand their power and influence throughout the globe.

8. Encourage every kind of domestic violence and confusion as American soldiers die in no-win wars in order to prevent the American people from seeing clearly what is happening.

9. Deliberately hand over Cuba to the Communists, thus establishing a vital beachhead for revolutionary action against the United States and other free nations in the Americas.

10. Plan to hand over the Panama Canal to Soviet puppets.

At the same time no move was made to get the Russians to give up any secrets, or territory, or to live in conformity with the United Nations Charter. And the Soviet regime has shown itself to be as secretive as possible, following in this respect the practice of the Russians from ancient times. Stalin often said, "I am an Asiatic," suggesting a Russian *Drang nach Osten* — a drive to the east — while keeping the Europeans at arm's length. But the appearance of the atomic bomb, with missiles to carry it to the four corners of the earth, has changed Soviet policy, except that much of the groundwork laid down by Stalin remains intact.

6

Whenever someone points out that 90 to 95 percent of Russian industry and technology were provided by the West, chiefly the United States, it is observed in rebuttal that the Soviet Union was the first to put a satellite (Sputnik) into space in 1957. Scientists and technologists generally agree that this was not very difficult, though it was a sensational feat. At that time the Russians had very powerful missiles because Stalin had seen from the beginning that, if the atomic bomb fufilled its promise and became the great new weapon, the Russians would need the power to deliver them within the United States. Such power was essential if only for purposes of extortion. Hence he ordered the Russians, with all the foreign help they could get, to develop a missile with the capability of hurling the bomb 5,000 miles and more. So for some years the Russians actually had more powerful missiles than the United States — a situation that might have suggested to many persons that the Russians possessed greater total strength than the Americans.

On November 25, 1971, the Associated Press issued a report from London that a Soviet space engineer who had defected to England had made a startling charge in a book published on that date in Britain. He asserted that "Moscow's spa^ program is a gigantic bluff covering bad workmanship and technical inadequacy." The news media in New York and no doubt in many other parts of the country did not publish the dispatch. Why? Because the same sources that had helped so much to build up the Soviet Union were not going to tear it down by publishing that unfavorable piece of information. The AP dispatch said:

> Leonard Vladimirov, a Soviet engineer and journalist, who defected while on a visit to Britain in 1966, said the Soviet space program originally began (in 1957) as a series of publicity stunts.
>
> In his book, *The Russian Bluff,* Vladimirov said these stunts were aimed at persuading the West that the Soviets had reached a high level of advanced technology comparable with that of the United States. Vladimirov's book describes political pressures and frustrations under which Soviet scientists and technologists work, always separated by security barriers. [Inside a Soviet factory or plant, this writer was escorted from one door to another with each door of each room being unlocked to admit him and then locked

again behind him. Reporters and others on one Moscow newspaper in 1972 had to take their typewriters to a closet where they were locked up for the weekend.]

Vladimirov said the West has always overrated Soviet strength in space because of early Soviet successes.

"Russia knew a long time ago that she could not beat America to the moon because she cannot build a moon rocket," he said. "Even today the Soviet Union cannot produce any significantly big jet nozzles."

Such nozzles, said Vladimirov, are essential to launch a manned moon flight. Vladimirov said that two- and three-men Soviet flights of the Voskhod series of the mid 1960's were short because the capsules were overloaded. He said the Voskhod spacecraft really were the older Vostok type with some equipment removed. Last-minute patching up of the modifications was a disgrace to engineering, he said.[5]

Is there any earthly (or lunar) reason why an American newspaper should not publish that piece? None except the reason already given. As a matter of fact, this was a fairly ripe piece of news that deserved a place on the front page. It would not have made Americans overconfident; it is doubtful that anything could, today. They would have digested it, and it would have helped them to get the Soviet Union into perspective. But, again, that was not and is not at all the plan.*

In regard to perspective, Dr. Antony C. Sutton, the preeminent authority on Western industrial and technological assistance to the Soviet Union, wrote the following in a letter to the author:

*Accuracy In Media, Inc. reported in its *AIM Report* of August-September, 1973: "*Jane's Fighting Ships* Declares Soviet Navy Most Powerful In World, But *New York Times* Keeps This News From Its Readers." This is identical with the deliberate omission of the news about the Soviet space bluff. In one case the Soviet Union was characterized as too weak to suit *The New York Times*; in the other case the Soviet Union was portrayed as too strong to suit the New York paper and its 362 client papers. AIM made this report:

"On July 26, [1973], *The Baltimore Sun* carried a front page story under this headline: SOVIET NAVY IS STRONGEST, JANE'S SAYS. . . .

"One of the world's leading authorities on naval power says the Soviet Navy with its own air arm and a greater range of submarines is now the most powerful

How To Construct An Enemy

In sum, the Soviets have great technical ingenuity and were working on atomic energy almost before the West. They published a number of key articles in the 1930's. They still have great technical ingenuity. However, they lack the technical *ability* to convert this scientific endeavor to practical technical systems — that's where Western technical assistance comes in. It enables them to convert their extraordinary scientific abilities to practical usable systems.

The massive transfers of industrial equipment and technological expertise to the Soviet Union from its founding to the present time indicates the vast gap between the abundance that a free society can produce and the poverty that is created by Communism. And the eagerness with which the individuals who control the destiny of the United States have actually served the Soviets indicates more than a desire to make a profit. The great weight of the evidence presented in this volume will show that the aim of the manipulators of our national and international destiny is the control of all nations through balances of power and internal checks and restraints.

There now can be no doubt that a highly organized and self-perpetuating conspiracy has been in existence for many decades — a conspiracy laboring assiduously to establish a global dictatorship and sure of its work every inch of the way. There are dangers in the conspiracy theory, to be sure; yet it is naïve to believe that the great bankers and industrialists of the United States and Europe have no understanding among themselves concerning what they are doing to expand and control their fiscal and industrial empires. Unfortunately, only the various tips of the iceberg have been seen.

---

navy in the world. Capt. John Moore, editor of *Jane's Fighting Ships*, writes in his first foreword as editor to the 1972-73 edition of the most authoritative annual on the world's navies, that the Soviet Navy had made 'staggering advances' in the last year.''

This report was top news by any standard. *The Baltimore Sun* story came from an AP London dispatch. The UPI sent a lengthy story about the startling assessment of Russian naval strength. It was front page news in *El Universal*, in Mexico City.

The New York Times, which boasts that it carries "all the news that's fit to print," told its readers absolutely nothing about this disturbing news out of London! Why??? The *Times* refused to explain the omission to AIM.

There are no public minutes of the meetings of the Bilderbergers, the Pugwash gatherings, and other secret conclaves of international personages. We can, however, clearly chart the course of the United States in relation to the Soviet Government by what has happened, knowing that it was made to happen.

For instance, it is not widely known that fifty top United States military intelligence officers, all with the rank of colonel or above, recommended that our government should discourage the Soviets from entering the Asian phase of World War II. It has been charged that General George C. Marshall, then Chief of Staff, ignored the farsighted recommendation, dated April 12, 1945, which read as follows:

> The entry of Soviet Russia into the Asiatic war would be a political event of world shaking importance, the ill effects of which would be felt for decades to come. Its military significance at this stage of the war would be relatively unimportant. . . . The entry of Soviet Russia into the Asiatic war would destroy America's position in Asia quite as effectively as our position is now destroyed in Europe east of the Elbe and beyond the Adriatic.
>
> If Russia enters the Asiatic war, China will certainly lose her independence, to become the Poland of Asia; Korea, the Asiatic Rumania; Manchuria, the Soviet Bulgaria. Whether more than a nominal China would exist after the impact of the Russian armies is felt is very doubtful. Chiang may well have to depart and a Chinese Soviet government may be installed in Nanking which we would have to recognize.
>
> To take a line of action which would save few lives now, and only a little time — at an unpredictable cost in lives, treasure, and honor in the future — and simultaneously destroy our ally China, would be an act of treachery that would make the Atlantic Charter and our hopes for world peace a tragic farce. Under no circumstances should we pay the Soviet Union to destroy China. This would certainly injure the material and moral position of the United States in Asia.

Yet even after Russia entered the war, just five days before the surrender of Japan, the Chinese Nationalist Government remained in power. And it would have so continued, but for a vicious betrayal by the United States Government. Indeed, it was General Marshall himself who arranged the destruction of the Nationalist Government on the mainland, and thereby made sure that the dire predictions of his intelligence officers would come to pass.

NOTES TO CHAPTER 1

1.   If the aim was only to make money, why was Russia strengthened by the handing over of Cuba to the Communists, with a loss of $3 billion in American investments and countless other material forfeitures? And why would we plan to give away the Canal Zone and the Panama Canal itself, in which United States taxpayers have invested nearly $7 billion? How does that make money, and for whom? The truth is that somebody is giving away the American patrimony, and doing it behind the people's backs.

2.   The Central Intelligence Agency announced on March 7, 1976, that terrorists might steal enough plutonium to make a bomb and hold an entire city for ransom to achieve their goals. Of course the CIA knew that Dr. Evans had warned of such a possibility twenty-five years earlier.

3.   On August 6, 1976, *The New York Times* carried, on an inside page, a story bearing a two-line, three-column headline: REPORT SAYS THAT U.S. CANNOT ACCOUNT FOR 2 TONS OF ATOMIC BOMB MATERIAL. The Washington dispatch said that officials of the General Accounting Office had reported that federal atomic agencies were unable to account for more than two tons of plutonium and uranium that could be made into "scores" of atomic bombs.

This report also said that an unclassified section of the report asserted that inventory controls were so inadequate that "timely response and recovery actions are precluded." The GAO had discovered that over the years the thirty-four federal facilities operated by the Energy Research and Development Administration (formerly Atomic Energy Commission) had been unable to account for more than 100,000 pounds of special nuclear material.

Only six or seven percent of that amount, it was reported, could easily be made into nuclear weapons. But that leaves 6,000 to 7,000 pounds, or more than three tons, that were usable for bomb production. Representative John D. Dingell (D.-Michigan) observed that only thirty-six pounds of enriched uranium or thirteen pounds of plutonium were needed to construct an atomic bomb.

According to the *Times* dispatch, this study dealt only with facilities operated by the federal government, and not with the fifteen civilian facilities licensed by the Nuclear Regulatory Commission to use plutonium and enriched uranium. Representative Morris K. Udall (D.-Arizona), chairman of the House Energy and Environment Subcommittee, commented disparagingly that some nuclear installations were "protected by as few as two guards armed with .38-caliber revolvers and shotguns."

4. The constant consolidation of Soviet power in Eastern Europe offers an ever-present threat to the nations of Western Europe. This too is a balance of power, in which the strength of the Soviet Union is weighed against that of Western Europe.

5. American superiority in computers for control and navigation of spaceships is given much credit among scientists for the first landings on the moon by United States astronauts.

CHAPTER 2

Starting A Balance Of Power

Man is not the creature of circumstances. Circumstances are the creatures of man.

— Benjamin Disraeli

DURING AND IMMEDIATELY AFTER World War II, machinery was put into motion in the United States to establish a worldwide balance of power weighted against the United States itself.[1] This was action without parallel in the annals of history. From time immemorial, governments and their leaders have sought balances that distributed power in such a manner as to protect, not menace, their own countries. In this case individuals and organizations within this nation have sought a "balance" that would give the Soviets a preponderance of power, and many specialists in the armaments field have concluded that the Soviet Union is indeed superior, if not supreme, in nuclear weapons.

There is no historical precedent for the deliberate self-stripping of a nation in order to give another country the power to establish a balance. It is just possible, of course, that America cannot make Russia strong enough, at least in the immediate future, for her to undertake the conquest of the world or to subjugate completely the United States in pursuit of such an aim. This is food for thought — and for satisfaction — despite the enormity of what has been done to America by its own government, with the aid of a large coterie of enemies, both foreign and domestic.*

---

*See *National Suicide: Military Aid to the Soviet Union*, by Antony C. Sutton.

THE BLEEDING OF AMERICA

As this is written, the United States is completing construction of the largest truck-manufacturing plant in the world in the Soviet Union. That should help to make Soviet Russia at last the strongest power in the world, at least putatively.[2] Its menacing power should then be adequate to justify additional measures of ostensible appeasement by our government, actually amounting to an increasing build-up of its strength. This build-up could in turn be used to force the American people to accept a condominium with the Soviets in a world government under the United Nations. That is the foreign policy of America, but not the stated Soviet policy. Presumably, the Soviet Government would be forced to comply with the directives of the *Insiders* who are guiding the foreign affairs of the United States and the United Nations. It should be remembered, first, that persons laboring to achieve these goals could work only in free countries; and second, that all previous efforts to arrange the affairs of the world by the redistribution of power have resulted in war. Contemporary efforts, including those of the Bilderbergers[3] and the Council on Foreign Relations, offer no real promise of world peace because those efforts are cynically aimed at the establishment of a global dictatorship over which the *Insiders* at the top of these conspiratorial organizations will preside.

Much of America's foreign policy has been undertaken clandestinely, with little public or Congressional consultation. While foreigners have been invited to participate in the formation of American foreign policy, and Americans have journeyed to Moscow in pursuit of that end, the American public often has not even been told what the basis of our foreign policy is.

After World War II the Soviet Union, through the machinations described above, was given the appearance of being a superpower. Stalin's strategy of working for hegemony over Europe and Asia was put into effect as he realized the real weakness and confusion of the West. His emissaries and allies in the United States and other Western countries kept him well informed concerning these problems, which they had helped to manufacture. Stalin knew that he had powerful friends in the United States — friends who had assisted him above and beyond the call of duty during the war. The Truman Doctrine did not pertain to Eastern Europe; and it was

14

never meant to include China as a non-Communist power. Moreover, after the delivery of China to the Communists, the Doctrine was relaxed in preparation for the Korean War, which the United States, fighting under the UN banner, was not allowed to win. Thus the precedent for no-win wars was established.

Although Washington accepted a stalement in Korea, neither the Soviets nor the Red Chinese were capable of holding out against the power of the United States. Communist China and Soviet Russia, which devised the war, were not ignominiously defeated and punished; there was not even any talk of expelling the Russians from the United Nations for their flagrant violation of the Charter. By that time it had become obvious to all that the Soviets had never intended to abide by the Charter anyway; and few other nations had any real desire to uphold it. Fifteen years later in Vietnam the Communists sought to push the no-victory attitude of the United States one step further — past stalemate — to defeat. Their allies in America clamorously maintained that the domino theory was fallacious. The truth is that it was all too sound, and the U.S. defeat deeply divided and confused the nation.

The no-win war is a most convenient tool for Communist expansion, but it is only an extension of the policy underlying all recent American actions, which is not to contest effectively the increase in Soviet power. The refusal of the United States and its Allies in the United Nations to win the war in Korea demolishes the theory — and the excuse — that the USSR might have used atomic power against us. Her atomic power then was dubious (as we will explain in some detail later in this volume). In no way did it match American atomic power. Thus the balance of power was deliberately established by transferring power to Soviet Russia. The decisive defeat of the Soviet Union and Communist China in Korea would have had the most favorable results for the United States and world freedom, but that was not in the game plan.

The aim of the United Nations in Korea was political rather than military. But it had no solid base, because the UN was not a united but a divided organization, created for just such treasonous purposes by high-ranking American participants in a worldwide conspiracy. Indeed, the Soviets used the UN to obtain war information which was passed along directly to the North Koreans and Red Chinese. This was well-known in Washington, though President Truman was surrounded by men who would hardly have urged him to take any action; some of them, undoubtedly, even withheld information from him. (Mr. Truman came only reluctantly to believe that Alger Hiss had betrayed his country. He never did understand the perfidy of others — Harry Dexter White, for example.) The Soviets were clearly responsible for starting the Korean War and continuing it to its inconclusive end. All the while, they were an active member of the United Nations. The Russians did everything they could to test the will of the West to expel them from the UN. From this, they learned that there was no limit that they could not exceed with impunity.

The present balance of power against the United States began with Lend-Lease to America's allies during World War II. Dr. Anthony Kubek in his powerful and scholarly work, *How The Far East Was Lost*, noted that during World War II President Roosevelt had ordered all United States agencies to ship supplies to the Russians before all other Allies. General John R. Deane commented that "the measure taken by the President was one of the most important decisions of the war . . . it was the beginning of a policy of appeasement from which we are still suffering." Dr. Kubek also observed that during the war, "with the enthusiastic help of Harry Hopkins," American Lend-Lease Administrator, the United States had shipped "millions of pounds of atomic bomb materials" to the Soviets.

Dr. Kubek recalled that in a book published in 1942 Dr. Nicholas J. Spykman of Yale University had urged a wise balance, saying, "A Russian state from the Urals to the North Sea can be no great improvement over a German state from the North Sea to the Urals." * Dr. Spykman also said that he felt the whole balance in the Far East should not be upset.[4]

But other far more powerful individuals in the United States had very different ideas about the new balance of power, which was

* *America's Strategy in World Politics: The United States and the Balance of Power*, by Nicholas J. Spykman.

to be created not *for the protection* of the United States, but *against* its best interests. *How The Far East Was Lost* also described the build-up of Soviet military and industrial might by the United States. Dr. Kubek cited the testimony of Major George Racey Jordan in regard to the shipment of materials for atomic bombs to the Soviet Union during World War II. Although the Major's important book, *From Major Jordan's Diaries,* created little stir in the East, on September 14, 1952, it received a powerful review in the *Chicago Tribune.* Here is a paragraph from that review written by Walter Trohan:

> It is a tale surpassing belief and one to make shivers race up and down the spine in contemplating the threat of World War III. The diaries of Major Jordan present an astounding account of arrogant Soviet connivance and of blind American trust, with ominous overtones of treason.

One wonders why other reviewers were not equally disturbed, instead of brushing aside this work as questionable. The truth is that for many years the atomic bomb was only rarely discussed by the left-wing national news media. Major Jordan received no Pulitzer Prize or George Polk Memorial Award, and no other public encomium, for his devotion to the interests of the United States. Nor did newspapers compete for the right to publish his book in daily installments so that the public would be widely informed of the existence and contents of this vitally important work. His diaries, therefore, failed to make any impact upon the nation. Major Jordan's only reward for his conscientious accounting of what was being shipped by air to the Soviets through Great Falls, Montana was removal from his strategic position.

Major Jordan had made a meticulous and extensive record of United States shipments to the Russians, for he believed that a scandal would eventually arise about them. He knew nothing about the Manhattan Project, or uranium, or any of the plans to create an atomic bomb. But he was a bulldog American, with great self-respect and boundless loyalty to his country. And from his experiences at the Newark Airport, the Great Falls air base, and visits to Alaska and Soviet Russia, he had gained a vast knowledge of what America was giving to the Soviets.

President Roosevelt had promised to give them "almost everything they want." Harry Hopkins went a step further at the Madison Square Garden Russian Aid Rally held in New York during June 1942, when he pledged, "We are determined that nothing shall stop us from sharing with you all that we have." When, at Newark Airport in May 1942, an American Airlines passenger plane accidentally brushed against and slightly damaged a medium bomber slated for delivery to Russia, the Russian officers stationed there were outraged. They complained to Washington, whereupon every commercial airline was ordered to cease activities at the Newark Airport for the duration of the war. Major Jordan wrote that he had to pinch himself "to make sure that we Americans, and not the Russians, were the donors of Lend-Lease." It was then that he decided to keep a diary.

Major Jordan noted that he "felt a foreboding that one day there would be a thorough investigation of Russian Lend-Lease." (The first complete study ever made of Lend-Lease and other transfers of goods and materials to the Soviet Union is Dr. Anthony C. Sutton's brilliant and comprehensive *Western Technology and Soviet Economic Development*, a three-volume work published by the Hoover Institution Press of Stanford University [1968, 1971, 1973]. The first two volumes drew a nearly complete blank in the American news media, with only two newspaper reviews — in the *Arizona Republic* and the *Indianapolis News*.) Major Jordan's *Diaries* and his statements preceding publication of that book did excite some Congressional interest in 1949. But the testimony of General Leslie R. Groves, who had been in command of the Manhattan Project, soon allayed that interest. General Groves had not been informed of the deliveries under Lend-Lease of vast amounts of atomic materials to the Soviet Union. The General agreed that the Soviets should be kept from obtaining the bomb, but when he publicly expressed this view, it was much too late.

We learn from the *Diaries* that as early as 1942 the Russians were receiving from the United States the materials needed to build an atomic reactor. Major Jordan provided a list of some of these materials, adding that he had not included in it "the millions of dollars' worth of mining, ore-crushing, and construction equipment" sent to Russia, and that informed readers might also find materials that could be used in the hydrogen bomb in other lists. He

Item	Quantity (in pounds)	Cost (in dollars)
ATOMIC MATERIALS		
Beryllium metals	9,681	10,874
Cadmium alloys	72,535	70,029
Cadmium metals	834,989	781,466
Cobalt ore & concentrate	33,600	49,782
Cobalt metal & cobalt-bearing scrap	806,941	1,190,774
Uranium metal	2.2	—
Aluminum tubes	13,766,472	13,041,152
Graphite, natural, flake, lump or chip	7,384,282	812,437
Beryllium salts & compounds	228	775
Cadmium oxide	2,100	3,080
Cadmium salts & compounds n.e.s.*	2	19
Cadmium sulphate	2,170	1,374
Cadmium sulphide	16,823	17,380
Cobalt nitrate	51	48
Cobalt oxide	17,800	34,832
Cobalt salts and compounds n.e.s.*	11,475	7,112
Cobaltic & cobaltous sulfate	22	25
Deuterium oxide (heavy water)	1,100 grams	—
Thorium salts & compounds	25,352	32,580
Uranium nitrate	500	—
Uranium nitrate (UO2)	220	—
Uranium oxide	500	—
Uranium, urano-uranic oxide (U308)	200	—

The total weight of the materials in this incomplete list is nearly 23 million pounds. And it should be remembered that Major Jordan was relieved of his post in June 1944, so that he was not in a position to ascertain how much was sent after that date, or what the grand total was. From that time to the present, the build-up of the

*(Note — "n.e.s." stands for "not especially specified.")

Soviet Union has been continuous. Lend-Lease and the Pipeline did the job until 1949, and they were followed by equally extensive aid and trade.

Fed up, finally, with persistent violations of U.S. immigration and customs laws occurring at Great Falls, Jordan went to Washington with the approval of Colonel George F. O'Neill, security officer at Gore Field. He received a rude reception, which spelled the beginning of the end of his assignment at Great Falls. After being shunted from one office to another, he finally was sent to John N. Hazard, State Department liaison officer for Lend-Lease. Mr. Hazard dispatched a young assistant to see Major Jordan. Here is the Major's account of the ominous insolence with which the young man greeted an officer who was fulfilling his difficult tasks above and beyond the call of duty:

> "Major Jordan," he began, "we know all about you, and why you are here. You might as well understand that officers who get too officious are likely to find themselves on an island somewhere in the South Seas."
>
> With natural anger, I retorted that I didn't think the State Department had any idea how flagrant abuses were at Great Falls. I said we had virtually no censorship, or immigration or customs inspection. Crowds of Russians were coming in of whom we had no record. Photostats of military reports from American attachés in Moscow were being returned to the Kremlin. Planeloads of suitcases, filled with confidential data, were passing every three weeks without inspection, under the guise of "diplomatic immunity."
>
> "But my dear Major," I was admonished with a jaunty wave of the hand, "we know all about that. The Russians can't do anything, or send anything out of this country, without our knowledge and consent. They have to apply to the State Department for everything. I assure you the Department knows exactly what it is doing. Good afternoon."*

But the tenacious and patriotic Major was not defeated. He bided his time. When, in May 1949, the nation was in a dither over the loss of an ounce of U-235 from the Argonne Laboratory, he

*From *Major Jordan's Diaries*, Belmont, Massachusetts: Western Islands, 1965 [1952], p. 112.

went on nationwide radio with the help of Fulton Lewis, Jr., later appeared before a Congressional committee, and thereafter published his diaries. Who will live longer in history and in the hearts of his countrymen, Major Jordan or the men who refused to do anything about the criminal abuse of the laws of our country? The Major said he had been "shocked at the efforts of the character assassins and press experts to keep the implications of this story from being brought into proper focus," but pleased that "clouds of witnesses" had come to his defense. Among those who vouched for his character, integrity and loyalty were Colonel William L. Rich, who had urged him to publish his diaries; Roscoe Turner, the great aviator; Colonel Harrison D. Blair, Paul R. Berryman, John Frank Stevens, and Colonel Theodore S. Watson.

It never ceases to amaze this writer that a person can be riding the wave of the present beautifully, and then suddenly, because he refuses to do something that violates every canon of his faith and loyalty, can become a virtual outcast until he can rally sufficient support for his cause. But as long as there is freedom, there is hope. Although Major Jordan did not live to enjoy them, honors and esteem are quietly and widely being extended to him today.

No newspapers, radio stations, or television newsgatherers had sought to check and confirm the Jordan facts and figures in Washington and thus establish the truth or falsity of these vitally important claims. But Dr. Sutton decided to do just that decades later, and he journeyed from California to the national capital for the purpose. In a letter to the writer in 1971, he said:

> Some years back I started with Jordan's data and attempted to run down the original Lend-Lease invoices to check out his figures. On the assumption that if he was right on, say, half a dozen figures —i.e., they tallied with the original official invoices — then we could accept Jordan's material. I had a job to get official Washington to find the invoices. With Congressional help I did it. Later I made a sample check and found that Jordan's data checks with the originals. *However,* there is still a vast amount of work to be done. Further, the key high-level documents are not declassified.

What is the stated policy of the United States in the matter of building up the Soviet Union? Although such a policy has been followed from the inception of the Atomic Age, it remained for Walt Whitman Rostow, chairman of the policy planning staff of the State Department in the Kennedy Administration, to codify it. Rostow prepared a foreign policy paper for President Kennedy, which was revealed and summarized by Willard Edwards of the *Chicago Tribune* in June 1962. Edwards wrote, in part:

> Rising tensions or the pleas of our allies or of the American public must be ignored in any crisis with Russia. The temptation must be avoided to prolong or expand any crisis in an effort to degrade or embarrass the Soviets in the eyes of the world.
>
> Gentle treatment of the satellite nations is advocated. No official attacks should be made against their regimes, whatever the provocation, and even criticism should be softened. Western Europe, at the same time, must be encouraged to closer relationship with the satellites and urged to furnish aid to them.
>
> Above all, no encouragement or support must be given to armed uprisings in eastern Europe.

This policy left the rest of the world as fair game for the Communists, while the U.S. was barred from interfering in their internal affairs. But Mr. Rostow went even further in formulating this arrogant policy, which would ignore "the American public" and tie the hands of the United States Government in any crisis with Russia. Incredibly, his foreign policy paper advocated the end of the United States nationhood, thus:

> It is a legitimate national objective to remove from all nations — including the U.S. — the right to use substantial military force to pursue their own interests. Since this residual right is the root of national sovereignty and the basis for the existence of an international arena of power, it is, therefore, an American interest to see an end to nationhood as it has been historically defined.

On March 30, 1971, Leonid I. Brezhnev, Secretary of the Communist Party and the actual leader of the Soviet government, said:

> In recognition of its international duty, the CPSU (Communist

Party of the Soviet Union) will continue to pursue a line in international affairs toward promoting the further activation of the world anti-imperialist struggle and the strengthening of the combat unity of all its participants. The total triumph of socialism the world over is inevitable, and for this triumph . . . we will fight, unsparing of our strength.[5]

That is fair warning, and nobody can say that Mr. Brezhnev has not been candid in offering a blueprint: "We will fight, unsparing of our strength," for the "total triumph of socialism the world over," which is "inevitable." There is no word from the Russians about giving up sovereignty and nationhood or about disarming themselves to the point of eliminating "national capacity to make international war." Granted that atomic war could mean an end of civilization, or at least the serious disruption of society for many decades, there is no reason to believe that our sacrifice of nationhood would remove the danger of holocaust after Moloch had been fed. At any rate, we would then no longer have any voice in our own fate. And the idea that unilateral disarmament would encourage the Russians and Chinese Communists to deal kindly with us is a dangerous delusion. Nationhood can never be abandoned safely in a world of nations, and even less in the face of aggressive nations with stockpiles of atomic bombs and a disdainful attitude toward rule by law.

And, argue as we may, history makes clear that a balance of power tilted against the United States was sought from the moment the atomic bomb was conceived.

NOTES TO CHAPTER 2

1. Medford Evans said in his book, *The Secret War for the A-Bomb*, page 53: "It could hardly have been supposed before 1945 that a great nation [the United States] would be intimidated by its own victory and, clearly alone in the first rank, would devote its diplomatic talents to the task of creating a balance of power against itself. It could hardly have been supposed that the inventors and makers of a revolutionary weapon would in the very moment of their triumphant discovery betray abruptly such signs of neurasthenia as, without renouncing war, to attempt to renounce their newest and most powerful instrument of war. The whole atomic policy of the United States since 1945 has been incredible."

23

2. By 1975 the United States was also building in the Soviet Union the world's largest computer plant, the largest fertilizer works, and the largest ship-building yard for oil tankers.

3. The Bilderbergers, an international group that takes its name from the hotel in the Netherlands where it first met in 1954, are almost totally unknown to the American people. The members are an elite group from the greatest industrial and banking countries, and they shun all publicity. The arcane conference is usually chaired by Prince Bernhard of the Netherlands. Americans who attended the gathering in 1974 included David and Nelson Rockefeller; General Andrew J. Goodpaster, Commander of NATO forces in Europe; Senators Charles Matthias of Maryland and Walter F. Mondale of Minnesota; various other representatives of the Council on Foreign Relations; and Helmut Sonnenfeldt of the State Department. How much of United States foreign policy is developed at these powerful and completely secret international gatherings has never been made public. The news media make no effort to cover the meetings.

Will and Ariel Durant, authors of the great eleven volume *Story of Civilization,* reached the conclusion that "the men who can manage money manage all." That distillation of wisdom out of a study covering some 3,000 years of human history should tell us at last where to look for the manipulators of our national destiny.

The *International Harry Schultz Letter* for mid-February 1975 said that the moving force behind political men is the big United States banks. Schultz asserted that this had been true for many scores of years, and that the political men were placed in position to carry out the policies backed by the bankers.

In his book, *The Federal Reserve Bank*, page 89, H.S. Kenan said: "The fact is that the top echelon of the Establishment is occupied by the bankers of the Federal Reserve System and a group of associated cartelists who intend to rule the world through the United Nations." He said that this "group of billionaires and their trained agents" were incorporated under the title, Council on Foreign Relations, which he described as "an international combine having counterpart organizations through Europe, Asia and Africa." He added that they controlled the world's wealth through their central banking systems and that they use this wealth and the people's credit "to advance their own objective."

Representative Louis T. McFadden (R.-Pennsylvania), himself a banker, asserted in the House of Representatives in 1932 that the Federal Reserve System was one of "the most corrupt institutions the world has

24

ever known." He said that it had "cheated the Government of the United States and the people of the United States out of enough money to pay the national debt," and he added that "the depredations and the iniquities of the Federal Reserve Board and the Federal Reserve Banks acting together have cost this country enough money to pay the national debt several times over. This evil institution has impoverished and ruined the people of the United States, has bankrupted itself, and has practically bankrupted our government. It has done this through the defects of the law under which it operates, through the maladministration of that law by the Federal Reserve Board, and through the corrupt practices of the moneyed vultures who control it."

4. Walter Trohan of the *Chicago Tribune* reported in his book, *Political Animals,* pages 221-222:

[Senator Burton K.] Wheeler came to [Truman's] desk before [he] went to Potsdam [in 1945] and warned him about Russian aims and intentions. Truman dismissed him by saying he could handle the Russians, but was concerned about the demands of the British and the French. Evidently the appeasers had got to the President first.

[Admiral William] Leahy was in the White House and accompanied Truman to Potsdam. He showed the President the forty-page memo [General Douglas] MacArthur had sent in advance of the Yalta Conference, which pleaded that Russia be kept out of the war in the Pacific.

MacArthur outlined the Japanese peace overtures, which I was to print later. These were (1) Complete surrender of all Japanese forces, (2) Surrender of all arms and ammunition, (3) Occupation of all Japanese homeland and island possessions, under American direction, (4) Japanese relinquishment of Manchuria, Korea and Formosa, as well as all territory seized during the war, (5) Regulation of all Japanese industry to halt present and future production of implements of war, (6) Turning over of any Japanese the United States might designate as war criminals, (7) Immediate release of all prisoners of war and [foreign] interests in Japan and areas under Japanese control.

Japan also sent peace feelers through Sweden to Russia. No doubt the Russians suppressed those they got, because they were aiming at getting into the war for territory.

Whatever the reasoning Truman chose to reaffirm the blunders of Yalta.

Mr. Trohan was a White House correspondent for thirty-eight years.

The terms he reports above obviously are those given to the Japanese and later accepted by them. Whether the Japanese were willing to accept them at the time of Potsdam (July 1945) is not clear. MacArthur's message on the subject could not be found in the Defense Department. Mr. Trohan said it was reported to him by Admiral Leahy. There is little doubt in the writer's mind (either Mr. Trohan's or mine) that Japan was interested in negotiating peace in the summer of 1945, *before* the atomic bombs were dropped on Hiroshima and Nagasaki. There is equally no doubt that the Russians wanted to get into the war at the last minute for territorial gain, though they were excluded from participation in the occupation and government of Japan. The balance of power at that time had limits.

5.   Brezhnev restated this position in his speech to the Soviet Communist Party Congress in Moscow on February 24, 1976.

CHAPTER 3

Building A Balance
Of Power

*What is the objective of the conspiracy? I think it is
clear from what has occurred and is now occurring: to
diminish the United States in world affairs, to weaken
us militarily, to confuse our spirit with talk of surrender
in the Far East and to impair our will to resist. To what
end? To the end that we shall be contained and
frustrated and finally fall victim to Soviet intrigue from
within and Russian military might from without. Is that
far fetched? There have been many examples in history
of rich and powerful states which have been corrupted
from within, enfeebled and deceived until they were
unable to resist aggression.*

— Joseph R. McCarthy
America's Retreat from Victory

*In brief, all presidential administrations, from that of
Woodrow Wilson to that of Richard Nixon, have
followed a bipartisan foreign policy of building up the
Soviet Union. This policy is censored. It is a policy of
national suicide. The reasons for it are not known.*

— Antony C. Sutton
National Suicide: Military Aid to the Soviet Union

THE BLEEDING OF AMERICA

IN ITS EARLY STAGES, this building of a balance of power against the United States went on without the knowledge of the American people, including even some of the highest government officials. It is interesting to note that this balance had its beginning in dealing with possession of atomic bombs, and it had become known to the public only when the struggle moved into the open. This came about through a statement by Dr. Leo Szilard, reported in *The Nation* in 1945. Dr. Szilard, one of the sponsors of the creation of the atomic bomb, had, under the leadership of Dr. Albert Einstein, joined in sending a letter and memorandum to President Roosevelt in 1939. (Actually the letter written to President Roosevelt was composed by Dr. Szilard but signed by Dr. Einstein.) Szilard played an important part in bringing about the construction of the bomb. He and Dr. Edward Teller, also a sponsor, were Hungarian *émigré* scientists who eventually came to a parting of the ways in America. Dr. Szilard was quoted in *The Nation* as follows:

> During 1943 and part of 1944 our greatest worry was the possibility that Germany would perfect an atomic bomb before the invasion of Europe . . . . In 1945, when we ceased worrying about what the Germans might do to us, we began to worry about what the Government of the United States might do to other countries.*

Coming from Dr. Szilard that statement was a shocker. For he was saying, in effect, that as soon as the menace of Nazism had been eliminated, even before the atomic bomb had been used and Japan defeated, the great danger to the world came from the United States. Szilard lost heart in the middle of the movement he had done so much to inaugurate. But Teller pressed on to become the father of the hydrogen bomb in the '50's. Szilard's words kicked off another movement that did not come to an end until the Russians began to explode atomic bombs, probably including some of our own.†

* *The Nation,* December 22, 1945, pages 718-719.

†The writer cannot forbear at this point to note that Einstein, father of the Atomic

Building a Balance of Power

That is the thesis postulated by Dr. Medford Evans in his remarkable book, *The Secret War for the A-Bomb,* which was published by the Henry Regnery Company of Chicago in 1953, after it had been considered by a New York publisher for several months. Dr. Evans, who received his doctorate from Yale University, writes in a vivid yet scholarly manner. His work is carefully reasoned, and every statement is backed by strong supporting evidence. But the new moralists in our news media ask of any work only, will it be good for the foreign policy that we personally advocate? If they deem that it is not — that is, that it will not advance their point of view — then they will not bring it to the attention of the reader, the listener, or the viewer. (Let the public take notice, and seek wisdom in the number and variety of the news sources it entertains.) So Dr. Evans' great work was not brought to the attention of the public in New York, or Boston, or Washington, nor reviewed throughout the country by *Saturday Review* or *Time.* Which is all the more reason for considering its findings in this volume. Only the bald will not discover it to be hair-raising.

In the early 1950's Medford Evans was the security officer of the United States Atomic Energy Commission. When his recommendations concerning protection of the components of American atomic bombs from theft were not accepted, he resigned. And he

---

Age and the chief sponsor of the atomic bomb, was excluded from official participation in the Manhattan Project because he was a pacifist in the 1920's. In fact, he had renounced pacifism in the 1930's, when he came to feel that it was one of the causes of the rise of Hitlerism. Yet he was asked for, and during the war he produced, a theoretical study of gaseous diffusion, which was an important phase of the Manhattan Project. "As a final irony," writes Ronald W. Clark in *Einstein: The Life and Times,* "a second memorandum which he tried to bring to Roosevelt's notice in March, 1945, included not only the suggestion that a bomb should not be dropped on Japan, but also the idea that the United States might build up an overwhelming superiority vis-à-vis the Russians." Of course Einstein was advised of the work on the building of the atomic bomb, but he, one of the greatest geniuses in the history of the world, went along with the gratuitous fiction that he did not know what was going on. It is not likely that he had any idea in 1946 of the plan to build up the Soviet Government to be a balance against the United States, or that he had the faintest notion that the United States Government during the war was sending large quantities of raw materials for atomic bombs to the Russians.

endeavored to tell the American people his vital story. It is from Dr. Evans that we obtained Leo Szilard's pronouncement that by 1945 the United States had become the greatest peril to the world. Freedom is indeed a many-splendored thing outside of Hitlerian and Soviet Hungary.

But Dr. Szilard carried all before him. He enlisted in his movement a great army of followers drawn from the arts, sciences, and professions, and even some businessmen.

Dr. Evans brilliantly and painstakingly traces the development of this movement until it ended in the probability that a considerable number of atomic bombs had been stolen from Los Alamos, Oak Ridge, and Hanford, Washington. There was no lack of documentation for *The Secret War for the A-Bomb*. Its authenticity was unmistakable. With even a little publicity from book reviews, this volume alone might have stirred the country to action. Instead it was buried under a mountain of silence.

James Burnham, a notable dissector of foreign affairs, wrote the introduction for the book. In a pellucid passage, he remarked that he did not believe that either Dean Acheson, David E. Lilienthal, or Thomas Finletter was or ever had been a Communist, but that it was a matter of record that all three "feared and distrusted the American monopoly of nuclear weapons, that they considered this monopoly a threat against peace and civilization, and that they wanted the United States to give up its monopoly together with its nuclear factories, its secrets, and whatever weapons were in its possession." And so, in spite of that record, "these three men — precisely these three —" were put in charge of the United States atomic project. Acheson became Secretary of State, Lilienthal Chairman of the Atomic Energy Commission, and Finletter Secretary of the Air Force.

It is noticeable that those who embraced the idea of a world in balance, with control of American atomic bombs given to international authority, were generally on the left side of the political spectrum. One American who advocated a complicated world balance of power was DeWitt C. Poole, an American diplomat, formerly counselor of the United States Embassy in Moscow. He wrote an article, "Balance of Power," which was published in *Life* magazine in 1947.* It is clear that he had been invited to write this piece to counter the views of *Life* publisher Henry Luce, who spoke of an American Century — one of American domination of world politics.

Mr. Poole urged the creation of a "world complex balance of power." He claimed that the concentration of power "at a single point," meaning in one country, was tantamount to "empire and tyranny." He said that a simple balance of power, "like the present one between the U.S. and Russia," did not serve peace. He advocated, therefore, the creation of six or eight centers of power, comparable in strength to the U.S. and the USSR but independent of them. He favored a federated Europe; a strong China under the leadership of Chiang Kai-shek; a strong, industrialized India; a revived Moslem world; a vigorous Latin American bastion linked with Spain and Portugal; a resurgent Britain; and an African federation. He maintained that a complex balance of power was "the only basis on which the U.N. could ever work."

Mr. Poole saw clearly that the creation of the atomic bomb made all the difference in the power structure of the world. He said, "The Acheson-Lilienthal-Baruch proposals were nothing less than a scheme for putting the balance of power in action. Our temporary and instinctively uncomfortable monopoly of atomic power was to be shared in such a way that no single power would ever again enjoy a monopoly." And with equal clarity he saw that Russia's refusal to help establish a world atomic authority had marked her as the principal enemy of such a balance of power.

Atomic fusion (and hence the hydrogen bomb) had not yet appeared in 1947 to further complicate the power scene, but when it did, it only compounded the problems. Mr. Poole made a valiant effort to solve them with his "complex balance of power" solution. While his suggestions appear somewhat more useful in retrospect, they were not accepted because this was not the predetermined game plan. His recommendation that the United States back Chiang Kai-shek and the Nationalists in China was eminently sensible. He apparently did not understand, as so many of us did not,

*September 22, 1947, pages 76-94.

that General George C. Marshall had already arranged the fall of China in 1945-46.

General Marshall received instructions for his China Mission in December 1945 from Alger Hiss, a Soviet agent in the State Department. That information was given to this writer by Robert Aura Smith, an expert on the State Department who was a member of the foreign news desk of the *New York Times* and the author of *Your Foreign Policy* (New York: Viking Press, 1941). It is convenient today to sweep many of these old problems under the rug as no longer germane to the kind of world balance that now exists; but to do so is to obstruct the establishment of historical truth. Then, if we come to a terrible fate through the clandestine actions of conspirators, the American people will not know what went into their undoing. (We will return to the subject of the invidious actions of our State Department in handing China over to the Communists, which already has cost the United States so much in Korea and Vietnam. But we will never understand our problems if we refuse to believe that Communists and their superiors in the conspiratorial hierarchy were involved.)

Mr. Poole felt that the distribution of atomic power around the world might somehow achieve what he called "a peace of freedom — an American peace." In the light of what has happened since 1947, Poole's views seem to be the height of wishful thinking. The giving of atomic bombs to ten power centers, instead of the seven — the United States, Great Britain, the Soviet Union, France, Communist China, India, and Israel — already known to have them, would reassure nobody in the world today.* Against his view, we must consider reality as it appeared to other students of foreign affairs, and in light of national purposes. This writer never believed that the Russians could be influenced by either appeasement or fear to halt their expansionist drive, which Russia has been pursuing for more than a thousand years, under Czars as well as

---

* According to a front-page story in the *New York Times* on March 16, 1976, the Central Intelligence Agency reported on March 11, 1976, that Israel had ten to twenty nuclear bombs "available for use."

Commissars.* Today Russia, with its dictatorial Communist government, is using allies and conspirators in every country in which a Communist party exists to advance its expansionist aims.

Look, for example, at the views of Arthur Koestler, a German who is a disillusioned former Communist and Comintern agent. In 1943, while the war in Europe was raging, Koestler wrote in his book, *The Yogi and the Commissar,* that Russia was the most vigorous expansionist force in the world. He suggested that the most vulnerable points for Russian attack would be the Middle East, the Mediterranean, and the continent of Europe. He asserted that the question as to how far Stalin intended to go was "naïve and meaningless," for, he said, a great power would enter contiguous and other vacuums until it met growing resistance. And he asserted that appeasement would not work in the case of Russia any better than it did in the case of Nazi Germany, for an aggressor who entered a "yielding environment" was bound to bring on war sooner or later through miscalculation. Koestler warned, by implication, that it would be a fatal mistake not to resist Soviet expansion, as the "balance of Europe can only be restored through a revival of the values on which Western civilization is based."

Koestler's book was written before the atomic bomb was known to mankind. Despite that fact, Koestler predicted the course of events with uncanny accuracy. The strange thing is that so many thoughtful men still believe that a balance of power will prevent wars, when throughout recorded history it has never done so. There was no precedent in history for a nation giving up enormous amounts of its own essential power in order to set up a balance with an avowed enemy, until that was done by the United States. The hope of mankind today lies in an appeal to all men to live by the precepts of justice and fair play, to respect the rights of men everywhere to worship as they please, to maintain a free and honest press and other media of communications, to ensure that elections are conducted fairly among an electorate informed and knowledgeable about the issues and the candidates, to demand incorruptible courts dealing justice with an even hand — in short, to preserve the greatest amount of freedom of every kind commen-

*See also Virginia Cowles's *The Russian Dagger: Cold War In The Days Of The Czars,* New York: Harper & Row, 1969.

surate with the public good. Meanwhile aggression should be checked the moment it rears its head.

Koestler was right on target when he said that appeasement would avail nothing. Soviet Russia annexed parts of Germany, Czechoslovakia, Iran, Finland, and Rumania; all of Estonia, Latvia, and Lithuania; Tanna-Tuva, the Japanese half of Sakhalin Island; and the Kurile Islands of Japan. Then she subjugated Outer Mongolia, Poland, East Germany, Hungary, Czechoslovakia, Rumania, Bulgaria, Albania, and North Korea. There have been a few apparent setbacks — if that is what they were. Albania apparently has broken away to become a partner of Communist China. Turkey rejected a Soviet demand that she cede the provinces of Kars and Ardahan. And a large area of Iran around Tabriz, annexed by the Soviet Government in 1945, was relinquished in 1948.

But the Soviet attack upon Greece followed in 1947, with the Greek Communist party forming a so-called Liberation Front (EAM) and a Liberation Army (ELAS) and fighting a phony "war of liberation." Indeed, the Communists, entirely undaunted by the sole possession of the atomic bomb by the United States, followed the same script later in Korea and Vietnam. And the Soviets also installed a Communist regime in China, with the help of the United States, which cut off all aid to its courageous ally, Chiang Kai-shek. Only the willfully blind refuse to see what was done to the United States while the Russians were doing what seemed natural to them by flowing into every vacuum.

The atomic bomb is not a weapon that can be entirely ignored in pursuit of a course of blatant aggression, even though the Communist Parties of the various countries were used as fronts and cat's-paws. When foreign party members got out of line, the Soviets administered swift and drastic penalties where they could. Since World War II, the Czechoslovakian comrades have been purged at least four times. On the other hand, when the Chinese Communists have failed to see eye to eye with the Russians, it has not been so easy for Brezhnev to impose "his" doctrine upon the Chinese; otherwise Red China would have been overrun long since. (The Brezhnev Doctrine sets forth the right of the Soviet Government to intervene when any of the "Socialist countries" takes actions not deemed by the Russians to be in the interest of all of them. It was announced at the time of the invasion of Czechoslovakia in 1968.)

The great traditions that have impelled the Soviet Russians forward, and the reasons they believe that they can move without fear of restraint, are graphically described in the *Russian History Atlas,* compiled by Martin Gilbert, a Fellow of Merton College, Oxford, with the aid of Arthur Banks as cartographic consultant. Once again we are indebted to the English for cultural probity and intellectual courage in the publication of this work. Nothing is omitted because of fear or for reasons of appeasement. This work spans nearly three millennia of Russian history — from 800 B.C. to the present.

The vicissitudes of the Slavs were great, as they were compressed or driven afield or subjugated by Asian nomads, Scythians, Greeks, Sarmatians, Romans, Goths, Huns, Avars, Khazars, Scandinavians and Norsemen, the Golden Horde of Mongols, Lithuanians, Poles, and Swedes. But all the while the Slavs managed to retain their identity as a distinct people, and after many centuries of vassalage they once again began to progress.

Then the Russians embarked upon their own campaigns of imperialism, in which they are still pressing forward to subjugate other peoples under the banner of "Communism" — or the false banner of "liberation" — to this day. On pages 109-112 of the *Russian History Atlas* are maps of the slave labor camps in European Russia, 1917-1936 and 1937-1957, and finally a great map of these man-made hells east of the Ural Mountains, 1918-1958. The text says:

Among the prisoners in the camps were peasants who had resisted collectivization, Soviet citizens who had lived abroad for any length of time (esp. Jews), foreign communists who had sought refuge in Moscow, inhabitants of the border lands (*e.g.*, Poles, Koreans, Chinese [and also Lithuanians, Latvians, Estonians, Ukrainians]), religious groups, state officials suspected of "sabotage," artists, writers, university lecturers, and leaders of minority groups (*e.g.*, Mongols, Uzbeks, Georgians).

That is a part of the picture that Arthur Koestler said the Russians would try hard to conceal. For those camps are still there, with far more than one million slave laborers, possibly as many as two to three million — many of whom are political prisoners.

Lieutenant General Leslie R. Groves was in command of the Manhattan Project from September 17, 1942, to December 31, 1946. He wrote in his memoirs, *Now It Can Be Told: The Story of the Manhattan Project,* that many persons now questioned whether we should ever have created the bomb, and that some had even asserted the United States was "morally corrupt" for having done so. And he added that, while the bomb had brought "death and destruction on a horrifying scale" when used at Hiroshima and Nagasaki, it *had* ended the war and thus it had prevented even greater losses for the Japanese, Americans, and British. (Presumably it was not known to him that the Japanese were already trying to surrender *before* the bombs were dropped.)

Moreover, Groves observed that it seemed certain atomic power would have been discovered anyway somewhere in the world in the "mid-twentieth century." He believed that if it had been developed first in "a power-hungry nation," that country would have "dominated the world completely and immediately." Thus General Groves believed that any totalitarian nation developing the atomic bomb would not have hurried to give away that vital secret, but rather would have proceeded to dominate the world "completely and immediately." Precisely. It is of only subsidiary interest that there was no major demand in the United Kingdom for the British to share their atomic secrets with the Soviet Government. The secrets in possession of the French probably were shared promptly with the Russians, as a result of heavy Communist infiltration of the French atomic program — an infiltration very similar to what had actually taken place in our own atomic program.

The Germans were far advanced toward creating an atomic bomb when World War II put an end to their efforts. In *Western Technology and Soviet Economic Development,* Vol. III, published on December 28, 1973, Dr. Antony Sutton reported on German atomic activity in the chapter entitled "Western Assistance to Soviet Atomic Energy." He found that German atomic efforts, from a scientific point of view, had not been inferior to those of the United States. Also, he reported that the Germans even then, before World War II, had been seeking to make a hydrogen bomb, and had conducted a number of experiments on thermonuclear fusion. So far as is publicly known, no work on the hydrogen bomb was done in the United States until after the war.

By the end of 1940 the Germans were producing a ton of uranium metal a month (maximum). At the end of the war they had seven isotope separation processes under consideration, two processes working, and operating equipment. They had built several subcritical atomic piles. The Russians captured virtually all of the German plants, metals and ores, and related documents, as well as most of the German scientists and technicians. All this booty was taken to Russia. Sutton asserts that it would be erroneous to believe the Russians did not obtain important atomic materials, equipment, data, and help from these seizures. He makes the point, however, that there had to be an important, and so far unrevealed, transfer of equipment and technology from the West to the Russians to enable them to create bombs, since the Germans had not been within sight of actually producing a bomb despite their progress in this field. Therefore, the Germans could not by themselves have given the Russians sufficient materials and technology to make a bomb.

Between November 10 and 15, 1945, President Truman met in Washington with Prime Minister Clement Attlee of Great Britain and Prime Minister Mackenzie King of Canada — "the three countries which possess the essential knowledge of atomic energy" — to discuss the atomic problem. They decided that responsibility for this weapon should be put "upon the whole civilized world." They recommended that the United Nations set up an atomic energy commission, where a world program could be devised. And so began the long search for world relief from atomic cares that was to end in the destruction of so many hopes — a Soviet veto. Stalin had remarked about this time, "We will have to have strong nerves," meaning that the Russians would outface the West on the atomic question. He was betting on a sure thing. The arms race is a fixed race — fixed against the United States.

General Groves makes it clear that a group headed by Dean Acheson, who then (1946) was Under-Secretary of State, was instrumental in setting up the panel headed by David E. Lilienthal that drew up a plan for sharing our atomic power with the Russians. This plan, which was in fact only a report to the State Department and the Secretary of State, James F. Byrnes, was leaked to the press, thus cutting the ground from under our chief negotiator with the Soviets, Bernard Baruch. But as it turned out, the Russians had never had any intention of accepting the plan, since they knew that they would get what they wanted by other means.

Released prematurely by the State Department, this document came to be known as the Acheson-Lilienthal Report. Its official name was *A Report on the International Control of Atomic Energy*. Despite its extreme generosity in proposing to build atomic bomb plants in the Soviet Union and elsewhere, it was rejected by the Russians because, according to Mr. Baruch, they wanted no part of an international system. Of course, the report revealed the hand of the United States and left Mr. Baruch powerless to bargain, even if the Russians had been disposed to do so.

Dr. Evans gave a vivid explanation of and commentary on the *Report* in his *Secret War for the A-Bomb*. There is nothing more fantastic in the history of diplomacy, and few men were closer to this fantasy than Medford Evans. He wrote that the Acheson-Lilienthal Plan was "admirably suited to Communist purposes," and noted that it called for the "construction and operation of atomic bomb laboratories all round the world in accordance with a principle of 'strategic balance' " that would bring other nations to a position of atomic power equal to that of the United States.

The *Report* itself says this:

> . . . At present, with Hanford, Oak Ridge, and Los Alamos situated in the United States, other nations can find no security against atomic warfare except the security that resides in our own peaceful purposes or the attempt at security that is seen in developing secret atomic enterprises of their own. Other nations which, according to their own outlook, may fear us, can develop a greater sense of security only as the [world] Atomic Development Authority locates

similar dangerous operations within their borders. Once such operations and facilities have been established by the Atomic Development Authority and are being operated by that agency within other nations as well as within our own, a balance will have been established. It is not thought that the Atomic Development Authority could protect its plants by military force from the overwhelming power of the nation in which they are situated. Some United Nations military guard may be desirable. But at most, it could be little more than a token. The real protection will lie in the fact that if any nation seizes the plants or the stockpiles that are situated in its territory, other nations will have similar facilities and materials situated within their own borders so that the act of seizure need not place them at a disadvantage.*

Thus, as Dr. Evans pointed out, Russia would be supplied with bomb plants, which she could seize and keep if she wished, while the United States could seize back the plants that it already had. A world Atomic Development Authority would have superseded national sovereignty in atomic energy matters — obviously an event that could only take place among nations that had shown the most scrupulous regard for treaties and promises. The Soviet Union hardly fitted the description. Dr. Evans remarked that when the Russians rejected the plan, "many Americans felt silly and ashamed, like a Puritan getting slapped by a demimondaine."

Only a nation in shock could have ignored Dr. Evans' truly brilliant work, especially in view of his sensational concluding suggestion that, if the Russians would not accept atomic bomb plants, we could give them some of our atomic bombs! The ideas expressed in the book seemingly received reinforcement both from Harry Truman, who had just stepped down as President of the United States, and later from the article in *The New York Times*, mentioned earlier.

The Russian refusal to accept the more than generous American proposals for an Atomic Development Authority was a blow to David E. Lilienthal, who had become Chairman of the United States Atomic Energy Commission in 1946. Lilienthal had

*Evans, *The Secret War for the A-Bomb*, pages 204-5.

already achieved some fame throughout the world by serving as the head of the Tennessee Valley Authority, a government enterprise created by President Franklin Roosevelt in order to stimulate a region industrially with power from the great Muscle Shoals Dams. Because Oak Ridge virtually was a part of the vast TVA, and perhaps for other political considerations, President Truman chose Mr. Lilienthal to be the chairman of an agency that was to develop a plan for dispensing United States atomic developments.

In Lilienthal's *Diaries,* he reported that Fred Searls, one of the members of the committee that drew up the Acheson-Lilienthal Plan, had recommended that a stockpile of atomic bombs be given to each nation, and that the United Nations should have some "bombs for retaliation." Mr. Lilienthal called that "one of Searls' gems."

Yet it is possible that, clandestinely, the problem was in part worked out in just that way. David Lilienthal saw and heard Soviet representative Andrei Gromyko in the United Nations' commission toy with and make propaganda use of the idea of a world Atomic Development Authority. It was a cruel first lesson in foreign affairs.

In January 1953, just one week after he left the White House, former President Truman told an International News Service reporter in Kansas City, "I am not convinced the Russians have achieved the know-how to put the complicated mechanism together to make an A-bomb work. I am not convinced they have the bomb."

Without doubt President Truman had learned a great deal more about Russian atomic capability since his meeting with Stalin at Potsdam in 1945. (At that time, he had been President for only three months.) In 1953 Mr. Truman was trying to give an important message to the American people. It had been he who, as President, announced to the world the first Russian atomic explosion in 1949. Now in 1953, when he could speak more freely, he was hastening to inform his countrymen that he did not believe the Russians were capable of making atomic bombs. But four years earlier he had been convinced that the Russians had produced atomic explosions, or he would not have announced them. Could it be that he was saying that the Russians had exploded atomic materials manufactured in another country — namely, the United States?

That supposition was weighed by Medford Evans, who had joined the United States Atomic Energy Commission at Oak Ridge in 1945 as Organization and Methods Examiner. Later he was transferred to Washington, D.C., and in 1951 he was named Chief of Training, in which post he was specifically requested to devote his time to security education and training. He resigned in March 1952, when he learned that none of his security recommendations was being followed. He concluded that twenty or more bombs, or at least the component parts, had probably been stolen from Los Alamos, Oak Ridge, and Hanford, Washington by 1949.

Dr. Evans cites at least two instances in which United States-produced fissionable materials were taken. In only one of these cases were the materials recovered. Allan Nunn May, a British scientist and a Soviet spy, confessed that he gave the Russians a vial of plutonium. Dr. Sanford Simons, who had no apparent connection with espionage, took a vial of plutonium from Los Alamos as a "souvenir," which he buried under his house in Denver because he did not want his children to touch it. His act was not discovered until four years later, when he was arrested by the FBI. There is no reason to believe that these were the only thefts of atomic bomb components. Dr. Evans says, "It is not at all improbable that unknowingly we have given Communists access to our most secret information and to the bins and shelves of our most remote storehouses."

Confirmation of this view is given by others. Dr. Walter Zinn, who was director of the Argonne National Laboratory, advised the Joint Committee on Atomic Energy in June 1949: "If you cannot have people who you are confident will not do this filching, your inventories cannot control the situation."

The first reported inventory of United States atomic weapons in 1947 produced a big surprise. *A Report of the Joint Committee on Atomic Energy,* which made an investigation of the atomic energy project, was released on October 13, 1949. Dr. Robert F. Bacher, who was head of the bomb physics division at Los Alamos when the war-time bombs were devised, made that inventory. He was quoted as follows in the *Report* (Page 13):

> When we took over in January 1947, as a representative of the [U.S. Atomic Energy] Commission, I went to Los Alamos to make an inventory of what we had. I made a rather complete inventory — this is at the end of December in 1946. This was directed primarily at making an inventory of the vital components of weapons, and fissionable material in our stock. This was not something which I or any other members of the Commission took lightly at that time. We took it very seriously.
>
> I spent 2 days as a representative of the Commission going over what we had. I was very deeply shocked to find how few atomic weapons we had at that time. This came as a rather considerable surprise to me in spite of the fact that I had been rather intimately associated with the work of the Los Alamos project — roughly, a year before.
>
> It might be interesting just to tell a word about how we conducted that inventory. I actually went into the vaults where material was kept and selected at random cartons and various containers to be opened. These, I then inspected myself, using suitable counters and other methods to determine to the best of my knowledge and observation that the materials were what they were declared to be.
>
> In addition to that, I was accompanied by Colonel [H.C.] Gee, Dr. [Norris E.] Bradbury, and other representatives of the various departments at Los Alamos, whom I questioned on every piece examined as to whether, to the best of their knowledge and belief, the materials were as represented on the inventory cards which we carried with us.
>
> Judging by the consternation which appeared on some of the faces around there, I concluded that this must have been about the first detailed physical inventory that had been made; and I think I can say without any doubt, that this was as thorough inventory as could be made without actually tearing things completely to pieces . . . .
>
> With weapons, the situation was very bad. We did not have anything like as many weapons as I thought we had, and I was very deeply shocked at what I found when I made an inventory of what we really did have.*

*Evans, *op. cit.*, pages 292-93.

Dr. Bacher also said, concerning the remedy for this situation: "Our first attention had to be directed toward the production of atomic weapons. . . . We felt it our first responsibility to do everything in our power to build the Los Alamos Laboratory. . . . I think I can say without being immodest, since most of the credit goes to members of that laboratory who went through that period, that success has been very marked."

Dr. Evans points out that, in atomic bombs, "whoever controls storage controls everything." It is impossible to ascertain accurately how many bombs may have been stolen, for a number of reasons. First, no one appears to have known how many atomic weapons were made and stored. Hence, there was no way to check. The presumption, however, is overwhelming in the direction of Dr. Evans' belief that some were stolen. When effective security is removed from as sensitive an area as bomb production and assembly, the theft of bomb components is not only expectable but almost certain.

In this writer's mind, there is no doubt that the Russians now have the capability of making and exploding atomic bombs. But there also can be no doubt that this capability was generated in the United States and other Western countries, and transferred to the Soviets in order to create a balance against the United States. Everything in this chapter and hereafter in this book can only indicate that this adverse balance was deliberately built and is being maintained to this day. The Russians therefore know that they have a built-in guarantee against overwhelming defeat in any conflict with the United States.

An addendum to this chapter appeared on page 6 of *The New York Times* for November 15, 1972, in a story headlined: "More Safeguards on A-Bombs Urged." It was reported there that Prof. Mason Wilrich of the University of Virginia had told the American Nuclear Society in Washington, D.C., on November 14 that the components necessary to make atomic bombs could be "diverted" from the increasing number of nuclear plants around the world. He said that the amount of nuclear material that could be used in explosive devises would reach thousands of kilograms in several countries by 1980 and would increase rapidly thereafter.

This news story pointed out that an atomic device could be constructed with a few kilograms of plutonium or relatively pure Uranium-235.

Professor Wilrich urged greater safeguards in the control of nuclear material to bar the construction of home-made atomic bombs by mentally disturbed persons, ambitious small nations, and gangsters. He said there was no "final solution for the nuclear control problem." It was an ambitious *large* nation that most probably first exploded "diverted" atomic bomb components.

Thus twice in 1972 *The New York Times*, nineteen years after the publication of *The Secret War for the A-Bomb*, published stories warning of the possibility that nuclear materials could be stolen and made into atomic bombs. Had the national news media brought this danger to the attention of the public in 1945 and the years immediately following, when this danger first existed and was becoming apparent to men like Medford Evans, we might have an entirely different world situation today. But, again, that was not the plan. Otherwise Dr. Evans' book would have been reviewed in New York, Boston, and Washington in 1953. Now that the planned balance has been established, the national news media is willing to talk about some of the nuclear dangers which still face us.*

---

*Administration officials in Washington reported on December 15, 1976, that the government had lost track of considerable quantities of weapons-grade atomic materials "leased" to about twenty foreign countries in the 1950's and 1960's, according to a *New York Times* dispatch. They refused to identify the countries. They also declined to tell how much plutonium and highly enriched uranium was involved. The information so far gathered was reported scattered through "handwritten ledgers" of the former Atomic Energy Commission; it was being recorded by the Arms Control and Disarmament Agency.

Weapons-grade material provided by the United States remains by agreement under its control. "But," said an American official, "if we don't know how much it is or where it is, we obviously cannot control its use." Evidently there was little inclination in the Washington bureaucracy to give more than lip-service to the alleged project to regain control of the lost weapons-grade materials.

Indeed, this kind of "news" in the papers has become so questionable that the reader is left to wonder just why it was printed: Was it meant to give information or to get a unit or units of the bureaucracy off the hook?

U.S. News & World Report on May 12, 1975, discussed the possibility that terroristic groups might gain control of some atomic bombs or the materials to construct crude but terrible atomic weapons. Dr. Evans had expressed great concern over this possibility more than twenty years earlier, but *his* very real concern was ignored because the time was not propitious. The controlled press had decided against such discussion.

On February 2, 1976, *U.S. News & World Report* reported that anxiety over the possibility of nuclear terrorism was growing in Washington. It said that one domestic intelligence expert believed that "a terrorist group will set off a nuclear weapon somewhere in the world during the next five years." *Now* it can be told. Why not earlier?

CHAPTER 4

The Soviet Union Minus The United States

Further, the distinction must be made between the Soviet system and the Russian people. It is easy to confuse an examination of this type with adverse reflections on Russian abilities. Such confusion would be grossly unfair. The Russian people have as much technical and scientific ability as any other people; indeed, in certain areas of science and mathematics they appear to excel.

— Antony C. Sutton
Western Technology and Soviet Economic Development

It may be unwise to attempt to read into an historical sequence of events as important as those described [the transfer of vast quantities of Western equipment and technology to the Soviet Union] any rational objective on the part of Western statesmen. Although the policies concerning trade and technical transfers appear vague and often confused, there is one fundamental observation to be made: Throughout the period of 53 years

46

from 1917 to 1970 there was a persistent, powerful, and not clearly identifiable force in the West making for the continuance of the transfers. Surely the political power and influence of the Soviets was not sufficient alone to bring about such favorable Western policies. Indeed, in view of the aggressive nature of declared Soviet world objectives, such policies seem incomprehensible if the West's objective is to survive as an alliance of independent, non-communist nations.

— Antony C. Sutton
"A Summation: Western Technology
in the Soviet Union,"
Washington and Lee Commerce Review, Vol. I, 1973

DR. MEDFORD EVANS SAID of the first two volumes of Antony Sutton's *Western Technology and Soviet Economic Development,* "This is possibly the most important book since the Bible." He said he had "thought a long time before committing that sentence to type," but he had done so because this great work "tells the truth about the umbilical relationship between Western technology and Soviet economic development." He pointed out that Werner Keller, a German writer, had tried to do the same thing in *East Minus West = Zero,* which, Sutton declared, "does not meet the methodological standards of the economist." Dr. Evans noted that he had sought to convey a similar message in his book, *The Secret War for the A-Bomb,* but that the towering achievement in this field is Sutton's. Dr. Sutton* has observed:

Almost all [of Soviet technology] — perhaps 90-95 per cent — came directly or indirectly from the United States and its allies. In effect the United States and the NATO countries have built the Soviet Union — its industrial *and* its military capabilities. This massive con-

* Dr. Sutton was a Research Fellow at the Hoover Institution on War, Revolution and Peace, Stanford University. Formerly he was Professor of Economics at California State University at Los Angeles. He has had experience in engineering and mining exploration in several countries.

struction job has taken 50 years, since the Revolution in 1917. It has been carried out through trade and the sale of plants, equipment and technical assistance.*

The Sutton work, which covers the years 1917-1965 and beyond, presents a breathtaking panorama of the transfers of Western machinery, technology, and personnel to Russia in order to make the Soviets into a strong enemy.

In describing the methodology of his work, Dr. Sutton reported that each plant was identified "and the origin of its equipment and technical processes traced." "This," he added, "was a complex and time-consuming task, involving a search in sources originating in a dozen countries." His primary sources of data were the U.S. State Department Decimal File and the German Foreign Ministry Archives for 1917 to 1930. The Western news media were another source; a third was Soviet trade representatives in Western countries — "a surprisingly lucrative source." Still another was the Moscow papers, *Pravda* (Truth), *Izvestia* (News), and *Ekonomicheskaya Zhizn (Economic Life),* and other Soviet publications. Miscellaneous materials in a number of languages — books, statistical summaries and handbooks — were also used.

In Volume I of his study, Professor Sutton examines the collapse and subsequent restoration of the Caucasus oil fields, noting that in 1900 Russia was the world's largest producer and exporter of crude oil. Nearly 50,000 feet of drilling per month had been necessary to maintain production. By 1920 drilling had dropped to 780 feet. "The Bolsheviks took over the Caucasus in 1920-1," he writes, "and until 1923 oil field drilling almost ceased." During the first year under Soviet rule, no new wells were produced, and after two years no new fields had been developed. An American company then came to the rescue.

To pay for concessions and agreements in the 1920's, when credit was not provided by a foreign company, the Soviet Government needed *valuta* — that is, dollars, other foreign currency, and gold. Of these only gold could be produced at home. A concession to Lena Goldfields Ltd., a British company, was signed on April

*Address to Platform Committee, Republican Convention, Miami, 1972.

25, 1925, to run thirty years in the Lena gold mines and for fifty years in the Ural and Altai Mountains. The company lived up to its agreement to produce more than 6,500 kilograms of gold per year.

To accomplish this feat, the company had to move to Russia from the United States a seventeen-foot Bucyrus dredge, which had been American-built in 1916 and stored in San Francisco ever since. The cost merely to move it to Siberia was put at $1.5 million. It was a massive thing, as high as a six-story building. Dr. Sutton writes:

> It was delivered to Lena in 1927 after being moved from South Milwaukee to Baltimore on 75 flat cars, to Murmansk (north of Leningrad) by steamer and to Irkutsk by rail, then 200 miles on a mountain trail by wagon and sledge, and then to Kachuca by barge on the River Lena. At Kachuca it was reloaded on small boats for a 700-mile trip up the River Vitim to Bodaibo, just 11 miles short of its final destination. Delivery and assembly took 18 months.*

Izvestia reported that by March 1929 Lena Goldfields Ltd. had invested more than eighteen million rubles in new equipment and had restored old works. But in 1930 the company was expelled from the Soviet Union, minus its dredge and other equipment. The company had been accused of using private prospectors and cartels composed of former hired laborers. "That this was the arrangement also used by the Aldenzoloto (Soviet Government) trust was not mentioned," Dr. Sutton remarked. And he added:

> In retrospect, there can be no other conclusion than that the Soviets deliberately enticed Lena into the U.S.S.R. to get the massive dredge installed and also as much else as they could along the way. It is, in the light of history, a clear case of premeditated industrial theft on a massive scale.†

Industrially speaking, expropriation of the property of foreign concessionaires seems to be the worst thing that the Soviets could have done. But they appear to have sized up each concessionaire and situation in advance, determined to get out of them just as

---

* *Western Technology and Soviet Economic Development*, Volume I, page 97.
†*Ibid.*, page 99.

much as possible. In one case they got a foreign company to mechanize production from low-grade deposits of manganese ore, while the Russians worked the high-grade deposits at lower cost.

Leonid Krassin, one of the early Bolsheviks, who were far less close-lipped than those who followed, said in 1921: "Russia cannot without assistance organize her trade. She cannot bring together her resources in a productive manner and she must rely upon capital, the experience and initiative of foreign capitalists."*

And that is what Soviet Russia did. The "capitalists" entered the U.S.S.R. like benevolent locusts. *Restoration* was the word. New railroads were built and old ones rehabilitated. Agriculture was industrialized, though only partially, and even then unsatisfactorily, for in agriculture were many factors initially involving private ownership and individual industriousness. Even today there is no certainty that the Soviets can grow enough grain every year to feed themselves. But at least the capitalists tried. Had their methods been adopted in entirety, there is little doubt they would have succeeded, as in the free countries. But that was the rub. The Soviet Commissars did not intend to allow any freedom to Russian farmers. In the United States in 1971 one farmer supplied himself and forty-four other persons with food, while the nation's farm population totaled a mere five percent of the total population. In Russia farmers constitute fifty percent of the total population, and each farmer feeds himself and one other — inadequately. This is also some measure of the technological gap in agriculture between the U.S. and the U.S.S.R. The Russian people spent 50 percent of their pay for food in 1971; the Americans (in the same year) only 16.5 percent.†

Dr. Sutton notes that the Western governments did not cooperate with each other in the matter of dealing with the Soviets, and thus permitted themselves to be played off against one another. However, they did see that the Russian Communists had abused foreign citizens by expropriating their property; that the foreigners' reward for honoring their agreements to operate concessions was to

---

Ibid., page 306.

†N.C. Brady, *Food and Life Sciences Quarterly*. (New York State and Cornell University Agricultural Experiment Stations) September 1971, page 3.

have their plants or industries seized when they were built.

In Vol. II of *Western Technology and Soviet Economic Development*, Dr. Sutton describes the continuing assistance of foreign companies in industrializing the Soviet Union, and the difficulty the Soviets experienced in digesting the enormous infusion of equipment and ultramodern technology. It must be remembered that a great number of Russian technologists fled the country or were imprisoned or killed during the twenties. Those who remained were so greatly distrusted that they were thwarted in their efforts, and often imprisoned or exiled. (Loyalty requires an act of will; it was servility — will-lessness — that was wanted. Dedication suggests an unreadiness to meet the new and conflicting orders handed down from day to day as they occurred to Stalin.)

Dr. Sutton explains the need for his monumental work on technology with the statement that a "State Department publication reviewing 40 years of Soviet economic development between 1920 and 1960 concluded that the U.S.S.R. has a self-developed technology. . . . There is then a problem of credibility," he writes. "A prime requirement, therefore, is to establish acceptability for the data and credibility for the conclusions [of this work]. This is particularly necessary because academic assessments, although accurate, have not been based on precise empirical findings but on more or less unsystematic reports and general statements. Further, the writer has used State Department files to establish a thesis apparently refuted by the State Department itself."*

In describing his methodology and data sources for this volume, Dr. Sutton writes:

> Details were obtained from several sources to determine both the technology used in Soviet manufacture and plant construction and its place of origin in the period 1930-45. For example, the Soviet standard blast furnace of 930 cubic meters has been identified as a Freyn Company, Inc., design. The turbines at the Baku Power Plant were built and installed by Metropolitan-Vickers, Ltd., of the United Kingdom. The merchant rolling mills at Kuznetzk were made and installed by Demag A-G of Germany. The coke ovens at the same

---

* *Western Technology and Soviet Economic Development*, Volume II, page 5.

plant and at Ketch were built and installed by Disticoque S. A. of France. The Karakliss cyanamide plant was built by Superfosfat A/B of Sweden. These and thousands of similar facts are precisely recorded and verifiable; the sources are always stated. Consequently those who wish to challenge the arguments have the initial burden of disproving recorded statements of fact.

. . . No significant new plant built before 1933 without some major Western technical and construction effort has been identified. Indeed, as Josef Stalin himself stated, two-thirds of all large enterprises built [in the U.S.S.R.] before 1944 were built with U.S. assistance.

By far the most important source of data is section 861.5 of the U.S. State Department Decimal File, from 1928 to 1946.*

It is interesting and significant that, as Sutton reports, the impact of foreign technology upon the Soviet Union was not investigated by the State Department, "although such an investigation would clearly come within the province of the Intelligence and Research Office of that Department." (As this writer observed in an earlier work, the truth is often hard to grasp, but it is never so elusive as when it is not wanted.) That Sutton leaned over backward to be fair and truthful is implicit in this statement:

A consistent policy of positive identification of foreign technology is retained throughout this volume. In other words a unit, process, or technology must be clearly identified from acceptable sources as being of Western origin before it is so named. In cases in which this cannot be done, the assumption is that the technology is Soviet. For example, the Pengu-Gurevitch process used in construction of a small lubricating oil unit at Baku in 1931-2 has not yet been positively identified as Western, although, given the nonexistence of Soviet developments in petroleum refining, it is unlikely that the process was purely Soviet; it was probably 'copied.' However, in the absence of evidence to the contrary, it is noted as a Soviet development. [Sometimes, as in the Ufa refinery complex, it is part Soviet and part Western in origin.]†

*Ibid., page 6.
†Ibid., page 8.

The Soviet Union Minus The United States

"Technical extravaganzas, such as Sputnik and Lunik, involving heavy investment in a narrow sector, are periodic stimuli intended to remind us that Soviet science and technique are, of course, far ahead of that of decadent capitalism," Dr. Sutton writes. "Those readers who have not forgotten the fallacy of composition might, however, ponder on the alleged quip from one Muscovite to another: 'Why, if things are so good, are they always so bad?' "

As those lines were being written the Soviet Union was receiving regular shipments of grain from the United States on a billion-dollar order. American farmers are always glad to sell their grain; and Americans as a nation are not inclined to gloat over the misfortunes of other nations. But it is difficult to overlook the fact that the Soviets' inability to raise sufficient grain for their own needs is hardly an indication of the highest technological capability — even though at the same time they are building what is alleged to be the world's largest navy and heaviest nuclear weaponry, and supporting wars and espionage in far-flung regions of the earth.

In an excellent book, *The New Tsars: Russia Under Stalin's Heirs,* John Dornberg reports of contemporary Russia:

> It is a country where flower shops have no flowers and butcher shops usually no meat, where queues and shortages are the rule. It is a land where portraits of Lenin and Brezhnev and yards of red bunting substitute for merchandise in shop windows, where stores either have nothing worth buying or are closed — "for repair," "for inventory," "for lunch," "for sanitation" or "for the day" simply because the staff has already overfulfilled its trade quota and sees no reason for continuing to work.

> Their restaurants display little signs in their windows that read "Closed" on one side and "No Seats Left" on the other, but never one reading "Welcome." It is a country whose economy produces envelopes without gum, elevators that don't elevate, locks that don't lock, doors that don't close, windows that don't open, refrigerators that don't refrigerate and new apartment houses that are instant slums before the first tenants move in.

This is Socialism? State capitalism? Sovietism? Certainly it is a combination of things. Every nation has its own distinguishing characteristics. The application of the terroristic political and economic philosophies of Marxism and Leninism to the country that was Russia did not then — or now — erase Russian and other national features from that land. Dr. Sutton discovered this as he peered deeper and deeper into the industrial structure. John Dornberg makes this revealing statement:

> A disillusioned member of the Soviet establishment once told me with considerable rancor: "It is a tribute to the greatness of the Russian people, almost a Russian miracle, that this country exists at all and that its economy functions, no matter how badly, despite fifty years of Communism. Russia was well beyond the takeoff point before the Revolution. Without this system we would be the richest, most affluent country in the world today."

That statement could be an exaggeration, of course, but the tribute to the great strength and endurance of the Russian people is deserved. Dornberg reports that Stalin's "regime of terror took the lives, by conservative estimate, of 20 million" — a figure that no doubt did not include the lives of the hundreds of thousands of Poles, Latvians, Lithuanians, Estonians, and other East Europeans — Hungarians, Bulgarians, Czechoslovaks, and Rumanians — who also died in the terror. He reported that a thousand concentration camps still continued to exist and that there were approximately a million prisoners, tens of thousands of them imprisoned for political reasons. Other sources have placed the number of political prisoners in the millions.* Despite the vast bath of materialism in which the country has been immersed for 55 years, belief in God and in religion persists, and is boasted of by the most able writers and thinkers. And one writer has said, "Russia's only salvation lies in a return to God."

With impeccable logic, Dr. Sutton argues that the transfer of technological capability to the Soviet Union was primarily responsible for the industrial growth recorded. In other words, no amount of investment would have been able to produce an automobile

---

*U.S.S.R. Labor Camps. Hearings before U.S. Senate Subcommittee on Internal Security Laws. Feb. 1-2, 1973. U.S. Government Printing Office.

before the car had been invented; but, conversely, a later model automobile or airplane or steel plant could be built even in a relatively backward country, given equipment, engineers, and freshly trained workers. That is precisely what was done in the Soviet Union. Therefore, Dr. Sutton argues, Soviet industrial growth is no enigma.

The true nature and extent of the buildup of the Soviet Union by the West can only be suggested in a chapter of the present book. Many phases of Soviet industry have not even been touched upon here. Military matters have hardly been mentioned. For instance, Dr. Sutton informed the writer that the Soviets could not have built an atomic bomb without certain machine tools that were obtainable only from the United States, the United Kingdom, or Switzerland. We reprint here, therefore, a speech delivered by Dr. Sutton to Subcommittee VII of the Platform Committee of the Republican Party at Miami Beach, Florida, August 15, 1972.*

The Case Against Red Trade

by Antony C. Sutton

. . . I am here because I believe — and Congressman Ashbrook believes — that the American public should have these facts.

I have spent ten years in research on Soviet technology. What it is — what it can do — and particularly where it came from. I have published three books and several articles summarizing the work.

It was privately financed. But the results have been available to the Government. On the other hand, I have had major difficulties with U.S. Government censorship. . . .

Almost all [of Soviet technology] — perhaps 90-95 percent — came directly or indirectly from the United States and its allies. In effect the United States and the NATO countries have built the Soviet Union. Its industrial *and* its military capabilities. This massive construction job has taken 50 years. Since the Revolution in 1917. It has been carried out through trade and the sale of plants, equipment and technical assistance.

*Quoted by permission.

Listening to Administration spokesmen — or some newspaper pundits — you get the impression that trade with the Soviet Union is some new miracle cure for the world's problems.

That's not quite accurate.

The idea that trade with the Soviets might bring peace goes back to 1917. The earliest proposal is dated December 1917 — just a few weeks after the start of the Bolshevik Revolution. It was implemented in 1920 while the Bolsheviks were still trying to consolidate their hold on Russia. The result was to guarantee that the Bolsheviks held power: they needed foreign supplies to survive.

The history of our construction of the Soviet Union has been blacked out — much of the key information is still classified — along with the other mistakes of the Washington bureaucracy.

Why has the history been blacked out?

Because 50 years of dealings with the Soviets has been an economic success for the USSR and a political failure for the United States. It has not stopped war, it has not given us peace.

The United States is spending $80 billion a year on defense against an enemy built by the United States and West Europe.

Even stranger, the U.S. apparently wants to make sure this enemy remains in the business of being an enemy.

Now at this point I've probably lost some of you. What I have said is contrary to everything you've heard from the intellectual elite, the Administration, and the business world, and numerous well-regarded Senators — just about everyone. . . .

First an authentic statement. It's authentic because it was part of a conversation between Stalin and W. Averell Harriman. Ambassador Harriman has been prominent in Soviet trade since the 1930's and is an outspoken supporter of yet more trade. This is what Ambassador Harriman reported back to the State Department at the end of World War II:

"Stalin paid tribute to the assistance rendered by the United States to Soviet industry before and during the War. He said that about two-thirds of all the large industrial enterprises in the Soviet Union had been built with the United States' help or technical assistance."

. . . Stalin could have said that the other one-third of large industrial enterprises were built by firms from Germany, France, Britain and Italy.

Stalin could have said also that the tank plants, the aircraft plants, the explosive and ammunition plants originated in the U.S.

That was June 1944. The massive technical assistance continues right down to the present day.

Now the ability of the Soviet Union to create any kind of military machine, to ship missiles to Cuba, to supply arms to North Vietnam, to supply arms for use against Israel — all this depends on its domestic industry.

In the Soviet Union about three-quarters of the military budget goes on purchases from Soviet factories.

This expenditure in Soviet industry makes sense. No Army has a machine that churns out tanks. Tanks are made from alloy steel, plastics, rubber and so forth. The alloy steel, plastics and rubber are made in Soviet factories to military specifications. Just like in the United States.

Missiles are not produced on missile-making machines. Missiles are fabricated from aluminum alloys, stainless steel, electrical wiring, pumps and so forth. The aluminum, steel, copper wire and pumps are also made in Soviet factories.

In other words, the Soviet military gets its parts and materials from Soviet industry. There is a Soviet military-industrial complex just as there is an American military-industrial complex.

This kind of reasoning makes sense to the man in the street. The farmer in Kansas knows what I mean. The salesman in California knows what I mean. The taxi driver in New York knows what I mean. But the policy makers in Washington do not accept this kind of common sense reasoning, and never have done.

So let's take a look at the Soviet industry that provides the parts and the materials for Soviet armaments: the guns, tanks, aircraft.

The Soviets have the largest iron and steel plant in the world. It was built by McKee Corporation. It is a copy of the U.S. Steel plant in Gary, Indiana.

All Soviet iron and steel technology comes from the U.S. and its allies. The Soviets use open hearth, American electric furnaces, American wide strip mills, Sendzimir mills and so on — all developed in the West and shipped in as peaceful trade.

The Soviets have the largest tube and pipe mill in Europe — one million tons a year. The equipment is Fretz-Moon, Salem, Aetna Standard, Mannesman, etc. Those are not Russian names.

All Soviet tube and pipe making technology comes from the U.S. and its allies. If you know anyone in the space business, ask them how many miles of tubes and pipes go into a missile.

The Soviets have the largest merchant marine in the world — about 6,000 ships. I have the specifications for each ship.

About two-thirds were built outside the Soviet Union.

About four-fifths of the engines for these ships were also built outside the Soviet Union.

There are no ship engines of Soviet design. Those built *inside* the USSR are built with foreign technical assistance. The Bryansk plant makes the largest marine diesels [engines]. In 1959, the Bryansk plant made a technical assistance agreement with Burmeister & Wain of Copenhagen, Denmark, (a NATO ally), approved as peaceful trade by the State Department. The ships that carried Soviet missiles to Cuba ten years ago used these same Burmeister & Wain engines. The ships were in the POLTAVA class. Some have Danish engines made in Denmark and some have Danish engines made at Bryansk in the Soviet Union.

About 100 Soviet ships are used on the Haiphong run to carry Soviet weapons and supplies for Hanoi's annual aggression. I was able to identify 84 of these ships. None of the main engines in these ships was designed and manufactured inside the USSR.

All shipbuilding technology in the USSR comes directly or indirectly from the U.S. or its NATO allies.

Let's take one industry in more detail: motor vehicles.

All Soviet automobile, truck and engine technology comes from the West: chiefly the United States. In my books I have listed each Soviet plant, its equipment and who supplied the equipment. The Soviet military has over 300,000 trucks — all from these U.S. built plants.

Up to 1968 the largest motor vehicle plant in the USSR was at Gorki. Gorki produces many of the trucks American pilots see on the Ho Chi Minh trail. Gorki produces the chassis for the GAZ-69 rocket launcher used against Israel. Gorki produces the Soviet jeep and half a dozen other military vehicles.

And Gorki was built by the Ford Motor Company and the Austin Company — as peaceful trade. In 1968 while Gorki was building vehicles to be used in Vietnam and Israel further equipment for Gorki was ordered and shipped from the U.S.

Also in 1968 we had the so-called "FIAT deal" — to build a plant at Volgograd three times bigger than Gorki. Dean Rusk and Walt Rostow told Congress and the American public this was

THE SOVIET UNION MINUS THE UNITED STATES

peaceful trade — the FIAT plant could not produce military vehicles.

. . . *Any* automobile manufacturing plant can produce military vehicles. I can show any one who is interested the technical specification of a proven military vehicle (with cross-country capability) using the same capacity engine as the Russian FIAT plant produces.

The term "FIAT deal" is misleading. FIAT in Italy doesn't make automobile manufacturing equipment — FIAT plants in Italy have U.S. equipment. FIAT *did* send 1,000 men to Russia for erection of the plant — but over half, perhaps well over half, of the equipment came from the United States. From Gleason, TRW of Cleveland and New Britain Machine Co.

So in the middle of a war that has killed 46,000 Americans (so far) and countless Vietnamese with Soviet weapons and supplies, the Johnson Administration doubled Soviet auto output.

And supplied false information to Congress and the American public.

Finally, we get to 1972 under President Nixon.

The Soviets are receiving now — today, equipment and technology for the largest heavy truck plant in the world: known as the Kama plant. It will produce 100,000 heavy ten-ton trucks per year — that's more than ALL U.S. manufacturers put together.

This will also be the largest plant in the world, *period.* It will occupy 36 square miles.

Will the Kama truck plant have military potential?

The Soviets themselves have answered this one. The Kama truck will be 50 per cent more productive than the ZIL-130 truck. Well, that's nice, because the ZIL series trucks are standard Soviet army trucks used in Vietnam and the Middle East.

Who built the ZIL plant? It was built by Arthur J. Brandt Company of Detroit, Michigan.

Who's building the Kama truck plant? That's classified "secret" by the Washington policy makers. I don't have to tell you why.*

The Soviet T-54 tank is in Vietnam. It was in operation at Kontum, An Loc, and Hue a few weeks ago. It is in use today in Vietnam. It has been used against Israel.

By 1975 the United States was also building in the Soviet Union the world's largest computer plant, largest fertilizer works, and largest shipbuilding yard for oil tankers. This illustrates the dovetailing of the policies of the United States Government with those of big bankers and a segment of big business. — H.H.D.

According to the tank handbooks the T-54 has a Christie type suspension. Christie was an American inventor.

Where did the Soviets get a Christie suspension? Did they steal it?

No, sir! They bought it. They bought it from the U. S. Wheel Track Layer Corporation.

However this Administration is apparently slightly more honest than the previous Administration.

Last December I asked Assistant Secretary Kenneth Davis of the Commerce Department (who is a mechanical engineer by training) whether the Kama trucks would have military capability. In fact I quoted one of the Government's own inter-agency reports. Mr. Davis didn't bother to answer but I did get a letter from the Department, and it was right to the point. Yes! we know the Kama truck plant has military capability, we take this into account when we issue export licenses. I passed these letters on to the press and Congress. They were published.

Unfortunately for my research project, I also had pending with the Department of Defense an application for declassification of certain files about our military assistance to the Soviets. This application was then abruptly denied by DOD.

It will supply military technology to the Soviets but gets a little uptight about the public finding out.

I can understand that.

Of course, it takes a great deal of self confidence to admit you are sending factories to produce weapons and supplies to a country providing weapons and supplies to kill Americans, Israelis and Vietnamese. In writing. In an election year, yet.

More to the point — by what authority does this Administration undertake such policies?

Many people — as individuals — have protested our suicidal policies. What happens? Well, if you are in Congress — you probably get the strong arm put on you. The Congressman who inserted my research findings into the Congressional Record suddenly found himself with primary opposition. He won't be in Congress next year.

If you are in the academic world — you soon find it's OK to protest U.S. assistance to the South Vietnamese but never, never protest U.S. assistance to the Soviets. Forget about the Russian academics being persecuted — we mustn't say unkind things about the Soviets.

THE SOVIET UNION MINUS THE UNITED STATES

If you press for an explanation what do they tell you?

First, you get the Fulbright line. This is peaceful trade. The Soviets are powerful. They have their own technology. It's a way to build friendship. It's a way to a new world order.

This is demonstrably false. The Soviet tanks in An Loc are not refugees from the Pasadena Rose Bowl Parade.

The "Soviet" ships that carry arms to Haiphong are not peaceful. They have weapons on board, not flower children or Russian tourists.

Second, if you don't buy that line you are told, "The Soviets are mellowing." This is equally false.

The killing in Israel and Vietnam with Soviet weapons doesn't suggest mellowing, it suggests premeditated genocide. Today — *now* — the Soviets are readying more arms to go to Syria. For what purpose? To put in a museum?

No one has ever presented evidence, hard evidence that trade leads to peace. Why not? Because there *is* no such evidence. It's an illusion.

It is true that peace leads to trade. But that's not the same thing. You first need peace, then you trade. That does not mean if you trade you will get peace.

But that's too logical for the Washington policy makers and it's not what the politicians and their backers want anyway.

Trade with Germany doubled before World War II. Did it stop World War II? Trade with Japan increased before World War II. Did it stop World War II?

What was in this German and Japanese trade? The same means for war that we are now supplying the Soviets. The Japanese Air Force after 1934 depended on U.S. technology. And much of the pushing for Soviet trade today comes from the same groups that were pushing for trade with Hitler and Tojo 35 years ago.

The Russian Communist Party is not mellowing. Concentration camps are still there. The mental hospitals take the overload. Persecution of the Baptists continues. Harassment of Jews continues, as it did under the Czars.

The only mellowing is when a Harriman and a Rockefeller get together with the bosses in the Kremlin. That's good for business, but it's not much help if you are a G.I. at the other end of a Soviet rocket in Vietnam.

I've learned something about our military assistance to the Soviets.

It's just not enough to have the facts — these are ignored by the policy makers. It's just not enough to make a common sense case — the answers you get defy reason.

Only one institution has been clearsighted on this question. From the early 1920's to the present day only one institution has spoken out. That is the AFL-CIO.

From Samuel Gompers in 1920 down to George Meany today, the major unions have consistently protested the trade policies that built the Soviet Union.

Because union members in Russia lost their freedom and union members in the United States have died in Korea and Vietnam.

The unions know — and apparently care.

No one else cares. Not Washington. Not big business. Not the Republican Party.

And 100,000 Americans have been killed in Korea and Vietnam — by our own technology.

The only response from Washington and the Nixon Administration is the effort to hush up the scandal.

These are things not to be talked about. And the professional smokescreen about peaceful trade continues.

The plain fact — if you want it — is that irresponsible policies have built us an enemy and maintain that enemy in the business of totalitarian rule and world conquest.

And the tragedy is that intelligent people have bought the political double-talk about world peace, a new world order and mellowing Soviets.

I suggest that the man in the street, the average taxpayer-voter thinks more or less as I do. You do not subsidize an enemy.

And when this story gets out and about in the United States, it's going to translate into a shift of votes. I haven't met one man in the street so far (from New York to California) who goes along with a policy of subsidizing the killing of his fellow Americans. People are usually stunned and disgusted.

It requires a peculiar kind of intellectual myopia to ship supplies and technology to the Soviets when they are instrumental in killing fellow citizens.

What about the argument that trade will lead to peace? Well, we've had U.S.-Soviet trade for 52 years. The 1st and 2nd Five Year Plans were built by American companies. To continue a policy that is a total failure is to gamble with the lives of several million

Americans and countless allies.

You can't stoke up the Soviet military machine at one end and then complain that the other end came back and bit you. Unfortunately, the human price for our immoral policies is not paid by the policy maker in Washington. The human price is paid by the farmers, the students and working and middle classes of America.

The citizen who pays the piper is not calling the tune — he doesn't even know the name of the tune.

Let me summarize my conclusions:

One: trade with the USSR was started over 50 years ago under President Woodrow Wilson with the declared intention of mellowing the Bolsheviks. The policy has been a total and costly failure. It has proven to be impractical — this is what I would expect from an immoral policy.

Two: we have built ourselves an enemy. We keep that self-declared enemy in business. This information has been blacked out by successive Administrations. Misleading and untruthful statements have been made by the Executive Branch to Congress and the American people.

Three: our policy of subsidizing self-declared enemies is neither rational nor moral. I have drawn attention to the intellectual myopia of the group that influences and draws up foreign policy. I suggest these policies have no authority.

Four: the annual attacks in Vietnam and the war in the Middle East were made possible only by Russian armaments and our past assistance to the Soviets.

Five: this worldwide Soviet activity is consistent with Communist theory. Mikhail Suslov, the party theoretician, recently stated that the current detente with the United States is temporary. The purpose of the détente, according to Suslov, is to give the Soviets sufficient strength for a renewed assault on the West. In other words, when you've finished building the Kama plant and the trucks come rolling off — watch out for another Vietnam.

Six: internal Soviet repression continues — against Baptists, against Jews, against national groups, and against dissident academics.

Seven: Soviet technical dependence is a powerful instrument for world peace if we want to use it.

So far it has been used as an aid-to-dependent-Soviets welfare program. With about as much as success as the domestic welfare program.

THE BLEEDING OF AMERICA

Why should they stop supplying Hanoi? The more they stoke up the war the more they get from the United States.

One final thought.

Why has the war in Vietnam continued for four long years under this Administration?

With 15,000 killed under the Nixon Administration?

We can stop the Soviets and their friends in Hanoi anytime we want to.

Without using a single gun or anything more dangerous than a piece of paper or a telephone call.

We have Soviet technical dependence as an instrument of world peace. The most humane weapon that can be conceived.

We have always had that option. We have never used it.

The preceding is the most eloquent and reasoned plea the writer has ever heard for a humane policy to bring the Soviets to a peaceful attitude, if that is possible. Yet this plea was totally ignored, even though it had been made available to the American press and other daily news media, including AP and UPI. It was later printed in both *The Review Of The News* and *Human Events*, two alert conservative weeklies, and in the *Congressional Record*.

Dr. Sutton mentioned, but did not stress the fact, that a peaceful Russian attitude could not have been the aim of the United States Government, because such an attitude was not sought. Indeed, pleas in behalf of working to achieve peaceful relations were ignored in Washington. *If it happens, you can be sure it was planned that way.* This great student of technology emphasized the role of our politicians and leading statesmen; but he is in a better position than most Americans to know that the communications media play a strong supporting role.

In spite of the magnificent reach of his mind, his incisive grasp of a vast subject, and the marvelous originality and clarity of his book *Western Technology and Soviet Economic Development* only two newspapers in the United States felt that they ought to discuss this work with their readers. Is it of any significance that the *Arizona Republic* and the *Indianapolis News* are published in inland cities? If so, why did not reviews appear in the *St. Louis Post*

Dispatch, the *Chicago Tribune,* the *Milwaukee Journal,* and the Dallas newspapers? And why is it that not a single newspaper on the East Coast or the West Coast reviewed a work of this significance?

The fact is, however, that Dr. Sutton is becoming a famous man throughout the country even in the face of this journalistic blackout.

CHAPTER 5

Mental Warfare Against The People

We find the communications media being used to undermine the credibility of everyone who represents authority, whether it be the government official, the business leader, the police, the school teacher, or the mere parent. In turn, the credibility of the media is called into question, and the public regards with increasing skepticism what they are told by the press and the broadcasters . . . .

It is shocking that in a society that has more motor cars, television sets, air conditioners, etc., per capita than any country in the world, the cry is going up that we cannot afford to spend the money required to provide ourselves with an adequate defense against our potential enemies. . . . This is not just the cry of some "lunatic fringe." It is a theme that is put forward by serious contenders for high political office. It is supported by influential newspapers and by some of the most influential voices heard on that powerful medium, network television.

— J. L. Robertson, Vice Chairman of
the Federal Reserve System's Board of Governors,
March 15, 1972

It is clear that the decline of a language must ultimately have political and economic causes.

— George Orwell,
"Politics and the English Language"

66

All of us who have had the duty of listening in the United Nations to the Soviet representatives are under no misapprehension. It is clear that the Soviet representative's recent speech abounds in examples of this difference in the use of words. All you have to do is know the language, what I may call the "upside down" language, of Soviet diplomacy.

— Foreign Secretary Ernest Bevin
of Great Britain in the
United Nations General Assembly, September 26, 1949

CORRUPTION OF LANGUAGE IS one of the legacies passed from the Soviet Union to the West. Having subjugated the people of Russia, the Communists were left with the stubborn difficulty presented by words. For words would not bend or yield. Hence it was necessary to change their meaning. If the West attacked the Soviets using damaging words, the Russian Communists would need to retaliate by turning the meaning around to favor them. Word meanings were changed, therefore, generally to imply the opposite of their accepted definitions. In the Soviet Government's dealings with the rest of the world, the Russian Communist leaders introduced virtually a new dictionary. They revised the definitions of old words and introduced some novel concepts with new ones. Their aim was to sow a sense of allegiance deep in the minds of Communists in foreign lands, while confusing non-Communist foreigners.

First of all, it was important to foster the concept that Russia was the citadel of Socialism and Moscow the Mecca of a new faith. Communists in other countries were told that they were holding on to "outposts." Until a nation had been captured by the Soviet Government and proper leaders had been installed, fresh from the Soviet capital or duly accredited, that nation did not belong to the Soviet circle. In the meantime a lexicon made in Moscow was imposed upon the Communists everywhere to bind them together and make them effective instruments. Since some Communists were to be found in every stratum of life in foreign countries, the new Soviet definitions were expected to seep into general usage. Which is just what happened.

67

Communists in other countries, especially the United States, rapidly got the idea and began on their own to pervert the words of their native tongues. Words, of course, are the warp and woof of communications — of news and views, of broadcasts and telecasts. The fact that the American communications media rarely mention domestic Communists does not mean that they do not exist. On the contrary, it was obvious to the cognoscenti that Communists had played a major part in the transformation of the American Democratic Party into a suicidal political organization in 1972.

There is now a "coalition" of Soviet word practices; some are used chiefly by the Russian Communists and some are featured by our own daily news media. This development presents a kind of preview of the global merger that the *Insiders* have in mind for us. A glossary of some upside-down words is given here as an illustration of this practice, rather than as a complete lexicon. Many other words will occur to the reader. Here is the list:

Activist: An agitator or fomenter of action; often a Communist. "Activists" shut down universities, burn sections of cities, work to destroy the morale of the U.S. Armed Forces, and provide aid to the Russian and/or Chinese Communists. But the media make no effort to identify activists as Communists if they choose to hide their party connection.

Advocacy Journalism: The deliberate distortion, suppression, or fabrication of news and editorials to push a point of view on readers, leaving out the facts on which to base reasoned opinions and judgments. It usually disregards American interests while pressing for clandestine world purposes that often coincide with the goals of Communist China and the Soviet Union.

Agrarian Reform: Empowering the State to redistribute land. The redistribution is everchanging; only the State's power to expropriate private property remains the same.

Bloc: An alliance of nations, such as the Western Bloc — which always is attacked by the Soviets. Never used as a term of opprobrium against the Soviet "bloc," as it is formed from ties different from those which bind the "Western" nations together. The Western Bloc includes South Korea, the Republic of China, South Vietnam, Japan, Malaysia, Indonesia, Great Britain, France, West Germany, Greece and Turkey, to mention only a few.

MENTAL WARFARE AGAINST THE PEOPLE

Capitalist: One who exploits others by engaging in private trade or business; an owner of any business or farm employing one person or more. One who shares in such a business. Also, one who believes in the free enterprise system. (*Capitalist* is an old word that formerly had a respected meaning. It was in use long before Karl Marx wrote *Das Kapital.* But nowadays few persons wish to be called capitalists.)

Colonialist: An advocate for or a participant in the affairs of a Commonwealth or any non-communist land that still has national ties with a mother country. The relationship between Moscow and the countries of Eastern Europe or the annexed lands of Estonia, Latvia, and Lithuania is never called colonialist. (Again, we see that there is one rule for the Communist nations and another for all others.) The word *colonialist* is meant to invoke an image of harsh treatment of colonies and their inhabitants.

Communist: A defender of the people.

Confrontation: Any national opposition to Communist countries and their satellites or partners. Unless Communist governments are permitted to have their way, the risk is *confrontation* — a nebulous condition that could mean anything ranging from a mere dispute to war. The use of *confrontation* as a tool of psychological warfare is a well-established practice.

Democracy (also known as the New Democracy and the People's Democracy): A collectivist dictatorship under which the leaders are imposed by Moscow. It involves single-list "elections" in which 90 (or more) per cent of the vote is given to the only ticket. Under such a system most of the freedoms set forth in the United States Constitution are non-existent.

Escalate: When a free country fights back against Communist depredations it *escalates* the situation. It is not possible for Communist invaders to escalate. The United States was frequently accused in the American news media as well as by the Communists of *escalating* the war in Indochina by fighting back against very real escalations of that conflict by the Communist enemy. But that is the way this one-way upside-down language works.

Fraternal Assistance: Soviet military invasion of another country to enforce dependence.

Imperialism: Any effort by a non-communist nation to aid another nation, or to trade with it, seek payment from it, enter into a military compact with it, or assist it in preventing the imposition of a Communist goverment. (Any or all of these definitions may be used as the occasion requires.) Also, any form of colonialism except that which is practised by the Soviet Government. Annexation of territory by any nation other than the U.S.S.R.

Kulak: A peasant or farmer who makes a living for himself and his family through his own husbandry, management, foresight, and individual planning. Such a man and his family are dangerous to the State since private farming cannot be coordinated into a totalitarian system. Only the most poverty-stricken farmers are to be considered non-kulaks. (The word *kulak* is seldom seen or heard nowadays, perhaps because the Communists do not want to call attention to the fact that Soviet and Chinese Communist farm systems regularly do not produce enough grain for those nations.)

Liberation: Enslavement of a nation by the imposition of Communism upon it. The process consists of infiltration, assassination, sabotage, and the setting up of phony shadow governments and armies that may or may not contain traitors from the invaded country. Thus, the Russians, Chinese Communists and North Vietnamese Communists have *liberated* South Vietnam.

McCarthyism: Any attack on Communists or Communism, including disagreements with liberals or pro-Communists. It is a fog word used to cloud issues concerning the Soviet Government, Communism, liberalism, and nearly any matter of import to the Communists.

The *Freeman* magazine reported in 1953 that the word *McCarthyism* was "first used by Owen Lattimore on May 4, 1950 in his testimony before the Tydings Committee [of the United States Senate]." Lattimore was close to the Soviets, the Chinese Communists, and domestic Reds in the United States. The *Freeman* article continued:

"The following day, May 5, 1950, an article appeared in the *Daily Worker* [Communist newspaper, now defunct] by Adam Lapin, political editor, using '*McCarthyism*' in the headline and text. Whether the *Daily Worker* got it from Lattimore or Lattimore from the *Daily Worker*, or whether both were suddenly and coincidentally inspired on the same day, we do not pretend to know."

It was precisely because Joseph R. McCarthy was right on target that he was attacked so scathingly by the left-wing press, pro-Soviet politicians, opportunistic public officials, and the hidden manipulators of world affairs. Nearly all the news media seized upon it. It was backed up by books and articles in nationally respected magazines. Intelligent persons today understand that McCarthy sought answers to the pressing question of why America, the strongest nation in history, was constantly losing ground to the Russians. McCarthy threw such fear into the Communists and their superiors that they continue to attack him.

Senator McCarthy's book, *America's Retreat From Victory,* which dealt with the disastrous decisions made by General George C. Marshall, contains many solid and irrefutable charges. Surely the creation of Communist China by the United States under the direction of George Marshall is one of the darkest episodes in our history. But McCarthy ran into a veritable avalanche of suspicion and abuse created by the men of the Left, and his body was overwhelmed by it. His memory is still under attack. But his spirit, his strength, his belief in America, his unwavering faith keep marching on. He will long be remembered by his countrymen, and his fight will go on.

McCarthy defined Communism as "a drive for power by a disciplined minority with welfare as its cloak." He declared that "Nazism was an enterprise of gutter intellectuals to gain the power of a great state and then of Europe." Now that McCarthy is dead, "McCarthyism" is used to smear others who would expose the Communists and those who direct them.

Patriot: A Communist. Also a "fellow traveler," that is, one who helps a Communist in party activities. (The word patriot is out of style in America, where it might be considered an embarrassment to the Communists and also, believe it or not, an "incitement" to Americans. The true meaning of the word needs once again to be taught in homes, churches, and schools, and to be enshrined in the hearts of all Americans who believe in freedom, including the Armed Services.

Peace: Absence of interference with Communists as they make war. Also, the absence of resistance to Communists as they take over a country. The word has no reference to peace as Americans understand it.

People's: A synonym for Communist; used to describe governments — as the *People's* Republic of China, the *People's* Republic of Bulgaria, the *People's* Republic of Congo, the Hungarian *People's* Republic, etc. Actually the people are very much out of the picture in People's Republics.

Picketing: A parade or demonstration by workers or other citizens;

not permitted in Russia but insisted upon by Communists elsewhere as an indispensable basis of democracy. Often carried on in front of the White House by American Communists desiring sure-fire publicity, but unheard of as a method of pressuring the Kremlin.

Reactionary: An intransigent non-Communist or anti-Communist; one who disagrees with Soviet methods, plans, or purposes; a capitalist; also a classical liberal, Fascist, or individualist.

Red-Baiter: One who attacks Communists; questions them or wishes to discuss Communism openly; believes the Soviet Government should abide by the same rules as other governments; feels that Communists should avow their creed openly; writes an unfavorable novel, play, or tract about Russians or Communists. (A prominent New York book critic condemned a novel by Mark Aldanov as "Red-baiting.")

Sovereignty: Traditionally, the independence, right of self-government, and territorial integrity of free nations. As used by Communists, it refers to the sovereignty of the U.S.S.R. and its right to dominate the slave states in Eastern Europe such as Poland, Rumania, Hungary, Bulgaria, and Czechoslovakia.

Strike: A work stoppage in capitalist countries for the purpose of bringing about increases in wages and/or improvements in working conditions; a way of demonstrating any labor grievance. Not permitted in the Soviet Union, but regularly used by Communists outside of Russia for political purposes.

Trade Unions: In the Soviet Union, organizations set up by the Government to channel off labor complaints; dues are compulsory; no action not sanctioned by the government is permitted. In capitalist countries, trade unions theoretically are kept free from any government control or regulation. They offer a fertile field for Communist infiltration for agitation, indoctrination, and funds.

Traitor: One who is disloyal to the world communist movement. Over the years the word has been used to describe persons who were loyal to and worked for some special goal of the free world.

Treason: The customary definition of *treason* is an act of perfidy against one's own country. But *treason* is what Communist instructions from Moscow require of their agents in foreign lands in the event of a conflict involving Russia. The aim is to introduce a sense of guilt or crime in these agents in order to bring about their complete subservience.

Value Judgment: An opinion, preconception, or prejudice; often used in contemporary journalism.

Warmonger: One who discusses Soviet aggression and considers means to halt it.

War Hysteria: The mention of Soviet aggression and conquest. Measures taken by non-Soviet countries to protect themselves against such capture.

World Opinion: A nonexistent, imaginary condition of global thought; the word is used almost exclusively in the free world as a tool to frighten the people and set them against some move that might prove embarrassing to the Communists; *world opinion* is another weapon in the arsenal of the enemy in the Cold War. The existence of this weapon is often denied by those who use it as an instrument of mental warfare.

The use of slogans is an age-old political device but the seizure and perversion of words on a wholesale scale is something new in international policy. The writer was once cautioned against using the word *progressive* loosely; he was told that the Communists had "captured" the word. On the other hand, the word *conspiracy*, in reference to world affairs, has been banned as a plague-carrier by the Establishment media.

Edward Hunter, author of the famous books on brainwashing, commented in his magazine *Tactics* on June 20, 1972, on the non-use of words. He observed:

Use of the words "conspiracy" and "treason" in reference to Communist and Communist-type attacks on the United States and U.S. interests has been practically banned because of an evasionary tactic that exploits prestige values. *This* has been especially effective in intellectual circles. You are a "low-brow" and called stupid if you talk about conspiracy and treason, no matter how obvious and proven they are.

This prestige tactic has been particularly effective in so-called intellectual circles that operate through the press, schools and churches. . . .

This has been a success in psychological warfare second only to the use of the term *McCarthyism* to prevent any criticism of Communism, no matter how mild or accurate . . . .

> There is a conspiracy to confuse, weaken, paralyze and destroy
> the United States on behalf of the enemy. Participation in this is
> treason, for we are in a state of war . . . .
>
> What has been allowed to develop is an area of privileged
> treason.

This chapter's exposition on how planned confusion is
brought about through the misuse and non-use of words would not
be complete without mention of Gary Allen's observation, "Communism, or more accurately, socialism, is not a movement of the
downtrodden masses, but of the economic elite."* It is this elite, of
course, which controls and operates the communications media. It
is not the people but the Communists and their supporters, lackeys,
flunkies and hangers-on who run the "People's Republics" — the
role usually given to Communist dictatorships.

British Major General J. F. C. Fuller, in a pamphlet titled
Russia Is Not Invincible, discusses the vitiation of words by the
Soviets and then remarks:

> Why has this policy of confounding the meaning of words been
> adopted? The answer is, that the nations "may not understand one
> another's speech." It is the story of the Tower of Babel bolshevized.
>
> The very name the Russian Empire now bears — namely, Union
> of Soviet Socialist Republics — is a lie; for the U.S.S.R. is not a
> union of republics as it is proclaimed to be; instead it is the com-
> pulsory serfdom of nearly two hundred subjugated peoples (national
> groups), speaking different languages and stemming from different
> cultures, each one trampled upon and held in leash by terror. Yet in
> this there is nothing new, for as the Pan-Slavism of Czarist Russia
> was but a catchword for Russian Imperialism, so today Communism
> is but the catchword for Bolshevik Imperialism — the most ruthless
> the world has ever known.
>
> Therefore, Communism is also a lie; it is but Marxian grease
> paint superimposed on a fundamentally unchanged historic Russian
> physiognomy. Though it is true that, in 1917, Lenin had produced
> such confusion that to save himself he introduced his New Economic
> Policy. It was out of his failure and not out of his success that, under
> Stalin, there emerged a mixture of state capitalism and Asiatic

None Dare Call It Conspiracy, page 33.

74

despotism which, depending as it did on slave labor, was so inefficient that it could not compete with the so-called "Capitalist" world — that is, with free enterprise. Therefore, in order that Bolshevism may survive, free enterprise must be destroyed. Today Marxist Communism is solely for export, because it is the solvent of free enterprise, and its precipitate is chaos, the prerequisite for the establishment of a pistol-ruled (Bolshevik) world.

Although that is what Dr. Sutton would call a general statement, it is nonetheless a keen and interesting observation. It came long before the belated but useful confirmation by Alexander Solzhenitsyn. It fits in with the findings of the Senate Internal Security Subcommittee in its *Report* for the fiscal year which ended February 29, 1972. That *Report* analyzes the several aspects of the program of the international Communists as follows:

(1) They seek to isolate America, to destroy our alliances, and to drive a wedge between us and our most important friends, West Germany and Japan in particular.

(2) They seek to disarm America, calling for a 75 per cent reduction in the military budget, the abstention from new military technologies, the curtailment of military research, the abolition of ROTC (Reserve Officers Training Corps), the liquidation of the CIA (Central Intelligence Agency).

(3) They seek to divide America by exploiting and exacerbating racial differences and minority grievances. Many of the grievances they seek to exploit are legitimate, and call for corrective action. But that the Communists are not interested in corrective action is apparent from their violent attacks on moderate leaders of our major ethnic minorities. Through the so-called "Black Liberation Movement," they fan the flames of racial differences and seek to utilize the ethnic minorities as instruments of revolution. [This is an old Bolshevik custom. It might be summed up in the slogan, "Use and abuse national minorities," since, when the Communists take over, all alike are submerged in the melting pot of serfdom.]

(4) They seek to further divide America along class lines and to undermine our economy by encouraging the most exorbitant demands by trade unions in which they have influence; by initiating wildcat strikes; and by an unremitting attack on the authority of responsible trade union leaders, mounted through movements like

75

the National Committee for Trade Union Action and Democracy, Miners for Democracy, and the National Rank and File Action Conference.[1]

(5) They seek to undermine our entire structure of laws and law enforcement — our courts, our grand jury system, the FBI and the local police. Among other things, they call for community control of the police, for "People's Tribunals" and for Citizens Committees of Inquiry.

(6) They seek to further weaken the authority of government and to give their immediate followers and allied extremists access to power, by agitating for community control of the schools, social centers, day care centers, etc.

(7) They seek to neutralize and destroy the two-party system by encouraging centrifugal tendencies within both parties.

(8) Operating primarily through the agency of Castro Cuba, the Tricontinental Organization, and the Venceremos Brigade, the world Communist movement seeks to sow chaos in America by encouraging, training and supporting the various American extremist organizations which are committed to a policy of urban terrorism, including the assassination of policemen and the bombing of public buildings.

(9) By attacking on all of these fronts simultaneously, the CPUSA (Communist Party of the United States) and the world Communist movement hope to bring about the destruction of "American imperialism," which they have proclaimed the "No. 1 enemy of mankind" for the obvious reason that only American power stands between them and their goal of world wide dominion.

Findings like these should alert thoughtful citizens. The warning should be taken seriously. We like to think it could never happen here. But so much has happened within our country and around the world that it should be a case of "Ten times burned, twenty times shy." Mental warfare is being waged in our country and everywhere else around the world. A balance of power imposed against the United States from within has consequences reaching far beyond those of actual physical confrontation. The adverse balance would cease to exist unless supported from within our country.

The effect is to downgrade the United States, its Armed

'orces, and its people. It results in playing Communists against
onservatives, totalitarians against Democrats or Republicans,
Negroes against whites, Northerners against Southerners, criminals
against law-abiding persons, draft-dodgers against loyal
Americans, youths against their elders, intellectuals against or-
dinary folk, West Europeans against East Europeans, the Soviet
government against the United States, the United Nations against
useful alliances and the free world, North Vietnam against South
Vietnam, Communist Cuba against the Americas, Nigeria against
the now vanquished Biafra, and the Congo against the late
Tshombe. Women's Liberation seeks to play women off against
men. Thus the division is complete. Men and women have always
managed; they face no great barrier. Some of the other divisions,
however, have had tragic results. The balance of power does not
seek a solution; it does not *want* one. It is a kind of world Don-
nybrook.[2]

A number of persons who have sought to play criminals off
against the law-abiding have been hoist with their own petard. They
have been victims of the very criminals they sought to use. Similar-
ly, others may well become victims of the world balance of power
that they have sought and were unable to control, as they attempt
to use terrorist forces against peaceful nations.

Until the people realize what has been done and is being done
to them, they cannot even begin to deal with the situation. It has
been accomplished largely by deception — deception of Americans
by Americans. The deceivers believe that deception can succeed,
can be covered up, only by more deception, so their falsehoods
multiply. But they should be beginning to understand that they
have reached the outer limits of the people's credulity. As the
deceptions become increasingly evident, as the people begin to see
the truth of what is actually happening to our nation, their desire
and ability to deal with the deceivers and the situation created by
them will grow correspondingly.

NOTES TO CHAPTER 5

. In an effort to undermine our economy, Leftists and their allies are

making inflation of our currency a positive policy. The prospect in 197
was for an inflation rate exceeding the 12 percent of 1974, when the deficit
laden budget of the Ford Administration produced its full effect. B
mid-1975 the United States Government had borrowed $197 billion sinc
World War II (nearly 40 percent of the total national debt then), not fo
use at home, but to be given as aid to foreign countries.

Inflation is one time-tested method of scoundrels for corrupting an
destroying regimes, as evidenced by many historical precedents, from an
cient Rome through eighteenth century France to Germany in the twentiet
century.

Just the interest paid on the national debt of the United States — mor
than $30 billion in 1975 — is a massive drag upon the nation's econom
and an enormous and never-ending burden upon its people, as no effort i
made to reduce the debt, rather only to enlarge it. In the second half o
1975 the national debt ceiling had reached $577 billion. (It is presently $70
billion.) The annual interest was approaching $40 billion. In the Federa
budget for 1976-77 the amount set aside for interest was $41.3 billion!

2. Another indication that the balance-of-power situation was comin,
full circle by 1975 was given by the Foreign Policy Task Force of the Coali
tion For A Democratic Majority. That group, headed by former Unde
Secretary of State Eugene V. Rostow, issued a statement early in the yea
urging a speedy redressing of the military imbalance (!) between the Sovie
Union and the United States. The Task Force said: "The nation is in grea
danger. Our danger is increasing every day. The Soviet Union continues t
pursue a policy of expansion that threatens our vital interests in Europe
the Middle East, and other parts of the world."

It said further that the "Soviet Union's expansionist foreign policy i
backed by a military building program which has no peacetime parallel i
world affairs." But it added that "our government continues to talk abou
'détente.'"

This was not a turning of the worm but a fundamental policy chang
in bud. The Task Force shrilly warned that NATO was being outflanked
that Western Europe was in danger of becoming another Finland, and tha
a similar fate could be facing the United States, the nation upon which th
future of the free world depends. Not a word about giving up our na
tionhood.

CHAPTER 6

War: The Bleeding Of America

We are not going to bomb civilian targets in the North. We are not using the great power that could finish off North Vietnam in an afternoon, and we will not. But it would be the height of immorality for the United States at this point to leave Vietnam, and in leaving, to turn over to the North Vietnamese the fate of 17 million South Vietnamese who do not want a Communist government, to turn it over to them.

— Richard M. Nixon
July 27, 1972

Nothing must be done to endanger communications between this country and the Communists. No reference must be made to Communism as the enemy. Furthermore this country is not striving for victory in the Cold War. The United States should not under any circumstances refer to Communist tactics as 'brutal,' nor should the word 'slavery' be used in referring to Communist takeovers of captive people.

— George W. Ball
Under Secretary of State in the Kennedy Administration

The peculiar notion of weakening ourselves while beefing up the enemy got started back in the days of Robert S. McNamara as an offshoot of more general theories about détente with the Soviet Union. Under the patronage of the Kennedy-McNamara regime, a group of left-wing intellectuals began cranking out studies which argued that we should build a "structure" of mutual trust with the Communists, reassure the Kremlin by pulling back on our forward defenses, and approach the goal of global disarmament by sustaining a "balance of terror" in which pervasive fear of nuclear holocaust would make the idea of scrapping military hardware seem attractive by comparison.

As set forth in a volume called The Liberal Papers and various documents produced by the tax-supported Institute for Defense Analysis, these theories converged in a bizarre doctrine of "mutual assured destruction" in which it was considered desirable that the Soviet Union be able to obliterate our cities, just as we were capable of obliterating theirs.

As Liberal Papers author Walter Millis put it, the end-product of such reasoning was the notion that a "genuinely deterrent policy would require the United States to cooperate with the Soviet Union in insuring that their retaliatory force was as invulnerable as ours and that our population was equally exposed to attack with theirs."

Though the idea was considered far-out at the time by Millis himself, it rapidly became converted into official policy through the efforts of McNamara and Kennedy disarmament guru Jerome B. Wiesner. In relatively short order the Kennedy strategists set about to build "structure" and reassure the Communists by signing the Moscow test ban treaty, cutting back manned bombers ["provocative" to the Soviets] and holding up work on anti-missile defenses. The thrust of our policy became to insure that our defenses were downgraded to signal our pacific intentions to the Kremlin, and led to such chilling furbelows as that reported by defense ex-

pert Donald Brennan, in which McNamara ordered that the Sentinel ABM have "some specific weaknesses introduced to make the system more easily penetrable by the Soviets."

— M. Stanton Evans

Sometimes in the past we have committed the folly of throwing away our arms. Under the mercy of Providence, and at great cost and sacrifice, we have been able to recreate them when the need arose. But if we abandon our nuclear deterrent, there will be no second chance. To abandon it now would be to abandon it forever.

— Prime Minister Winston Churchill

A CEASE-FIRE IN the Vietnam War was formally proclaimed at 8 a.m. January 28, 1973. By February 17 the Associated Press reported that South Vietnamese and North Vietnamese had suffered nearly 15,000 casualties since the "cease-fire." Some of this fighting was called the fiercest of the war. Fighting continued also in Laos and Cambodia during that time. The United States withdrew the last of its forces from South Vietnam on March 29, 1973. Within the year following the so-called cease-fire, the two sides in Vietnam had inflicted as many casualties upon each other as the number suffered by Americans in the entire war — more than 350,000.

Continued fighting after a cease-fire is normal procedure for the Communists. Nor would the conclusion of one war mean that they would not ignite another conflict elsewhere soon thereafter. (The Soviet Communists instigated the war in the Middle East in October 1973.) We are concerned here with history and the matter of getting it straight. Specifically, we are concerned with the bleeding of America in two great wars in Korea and Indochina. The two Vietnams, South and North, Cambodia, Laos, and Thailand

81

figure in the second war. A cease-fire was declared in Laos on February 22, 1973, but the fighting there continued. It went on also in Cambodia, where no cease-fire had been reached by mid-1974.

The Korean War was the second great post-World War II disaster in Asia, the first having been the handing over of China to the Communists. General Curtis E. LeMay, former Chief of Staff of the United States Air Force, reported in 1966 that there were 3.5 million military casualties on both sides in three years in Korea, "where we also pulled our Sunday punch. Over a million civilians were killed and other millions left homeless in this protracted land struggle," he added. "I can't believe that this is the most humane way to fight a war." Indeed it was not. But as it turned out, that was not the object. The object was to avoid embarrassing the Soviets and Chinese Communists by mentioning their involvement in the war; and to make sure that the U.S. did not emerge victorious. Undoubtedly, Joseph Stalin planned the Korean War, probably in collaboration with Mao Tse-Tung, who was in Moscow from December 1949 to February 14, 1950. The war started on June 25, 1950. The Truman Administration vociferously maintained the dual fiction that the war was initiated and prosecuted by the North Koreans without assistance or direction from their Soviet masters, and that the Chinese Communists engaged in the fighting as "volunteers." This fiction was maintained even though the Chinese were led by General Lin Piao, a top Red officer. (He became later the Defense Minister of Red China, and in 1970 was killed during an alleged attempt to flee from China to the Soviet Union.) On February 1, 1951, the United Nations General Assembly identified Communist China as the aggressor in Korea, not mentioning either the Soviets or the North Koreans.

This was typical of the way the war was managed by the United Nations — with a minimum regard for the obvious realities of the conflict. The Soviet Government, author of this war tragedy, was allowed to retain its membership in the United Nations. It even utilized the U.N.'s New York headquarters as a base for relaying the messages and plans of the U.N. Commander, General Douglas MacArthur, to Moscow. From there, they were sent directly to the North Korean high command. Finally, General MacArthur, one of

America's greatest military leaders, was dismissed by President Truman because the General sought victory in Korea. MacArthur bitterly charged that "Washington planning was not directed toward methods of counterattack, but rather toward the best way to run." It was only the beginning of the post-World War II physical bleeding of America, a curtain-raiser for the Vietnam War, which maimed and killed more than twice as many Americans.

A total of 5,764,143 Americans served in the United States Armed Forces in the Korean War — almost three million of them in the Army; nearly one half million in the Marine Corps; 1,285,000 in the Air Force; 1,177,000 in the Navy; and 44,143 in the Coast Guard. Battle deaths totalled 33,629. There were 20,617 deaths from other causes, and 103,284 were wounded. United States combat casualties in Vietnam totalled 46,520 killed, 10,389 dead from non-hostile causes (accidents and illness), 303,704 wounded, and 1,900 missing or prisoners, 560 of whom were released early in 1973. More than 3.3 million Americans served in Southeast Asia. The South Vietnamese battle deaths through January 13, 1973 were estimated at 183,528 and the Communist dead were estimated at 924,048. If there were four wounded for each Vietnamese death (a much lower hypothetical ratio than actually occurred among Americans) the total of North and South Vietnamese casualties (dead and wounded) would be more than 5 million.

The Korean "peace talks" lasted for two years (July 1951-July 1953), during which time the Americans suffered more than 70,000 casualties. The equally fraudulent "peace talks" on the Vietnam War began at Paris on May 10, 1968. From then till February 1972, the Americans suffered more than 181,000 casualties (22,000 dead)* during offensive after offensive launched by the North Vietnamese, and there were vast numbers of civilian as well as battlefield casualties among the South Vietnamese. Peace talks are strictly a bleeding operation with the Communists, who have no intention of reaching any kind of compromise. In spite of their protestations that their aims are benevolent, they show not the slightest regard for human life. If there is any of the milk of human kindness

* *U.S. News & World Report,* February 7, 1972.

in them, it was not revealed by any action recorded in either of these wars.

Conversely, the great sacrifices made by the nations of the West ultimately helped to build up the Communists in both the Soviet Union and Red China. Our national news media as a whole showed no great concern over the carnage. Although newspapers throughout the country printed pictures of Americans who gave their lives, the news media in New York — with the notable exception of the *Daily News* — treated the conflict as if they were being told to propagandize for the enemy. Indeed, it was the view of many U.S. military officers who served in Vietnam that this segment of the media was providing comfort and assistance to the Communists. There was never any doubt in the highest military quarters that the Americans alone could have won the war in a few weeks if permitted to do so. President Nixon himself said on July 27, 1972: "We are not using the great power that could finish off North Vietnam in an afternoon, and we will not." He claimed, however, that the United States was acting as humanely as possible.

The American communications media themselves were guilty of deliberately creating every excuse to throw obstacles that helped to prevent the winning of the war. Broadly speaking, they were guilty of the following acts:

1. A vicious and continued undermining of every government of South Vietnam, from the Diem Administration in the early 1960's to the Thieu Government in 1972. Problems in South Vietnam were usually attributed to the Saigon Government, not to the North Vietnamese invaders.

2. A blatant smearing of the South Vietnamese armies and people.

3. Defense of the restraining of Americans and Allies so as to enable entire battalions of North Vietnamese to escape and fight again, leading to thousands of unnecessary casualties. They opposed the use of any kind of gas to flush the enemy out of tunnels. They condemned search-and-destroy operations. They denounced defoliation as a means of exposing the enemy. They denied the enemy's flagrant use of Cambodia as a sanctuary for years. And they hysterically attacked President Nixon's drive into Cambodia, one of the most sensible military moves undertaken by the Allies in

Southeast Asia, which eventually saved the lives of many Americans and others. The media attacked rain-making as an alteration of the environment (never mind that it undoubtedly saved lives on both sides). They vigorously opposed the bombing of North Vietnam, even though the military was seldom, if ever, allowed to bomb effectively. Targets chosen by the military were in most cases put off limits by the Defense Department, under Robert Strange McNamara. When the North was being effectively bombed in 1972, a propaganda campaign in the United States was undertaken to stop it by calling it "dike bombing," though no dikes were targeted, and it is entirely possible that the damage done to the dikes was the result of North Vietnamese antiaircraft shells falling back upon the dikes and exploding there. Also, some dikes were damaged by floods. Later, in December 1972, very heavy strategic bombing by the United States was denounced as being directed against civilians and hospitals, though, strangely, dikes were not again mentioned. All these media attacks also provided the enemy with a propaganda lever.

4. Vast publicity for the My Lai cases, which involved Americans accused of killing more than 100 South Vietnamese civilians; meanwhile hundreds of similar actions, cold-bloodedly ordered by the North Vietnamese Government, were either ignored completely or played down. *The New York Times* at first gave little space to the gruesome murders of between 4,000 and 5,800 South Vietnamese at Hue in 1968, although it devoted entire pages to the My Lai cases, in which American soldiers were likened by *Times* writers to Nazis who had killed millions.

5. Reporting and playing up of mutinies of Americans on the battlefield as victories while desertions of South Vietnamese soldiers were cited as proofs of weakness.

The aim was apparently to blame the United States, to shame it, to prevent any victory, and to reduce its power, while the real culprits — the North Vietnamese Communist invaders and their Russian and Chinese Communist suppliers — were ignored. President Lyndon B. Johnson paid with his political life for refusing to win the war. And President Kennedy might still be alive if he had wiped out the Communists in Cuba. The American people always wanted to win the war as quickly as possible, thus saving lives on both sides. They wanted to follow the most humane, honorable, and sensible method for ending the conflict, since any other would damage our own country, and our ties and influence around the world. Even Americans with little knowledge of foreign affairs understood that.*

In the spring of 1972 President Nixon ordered mining of the rivers, harbors, and canals of North Vietnam, and the bombing of industrial and military targets there, in retaliation for the massive invasion of South Vietnam that began March 31, 1972. About 11,000 mines were dropped into North Vietnamese waters, coastal and inland, and strategic targets were bombed totally in 1972 and early 1973. This presidential action was in defiance of the idea often expressed in the American news media that such a move might bring on a general war with Russia and Communist China. (Earlier in the year the President had visited Mao Tse-tung and Chou En-lai in Peking. And a few months later he went to Moscow to sign a number of military and civil agreements, while the bombing of North Vietnam continued, and the rivers and harbors were still mined.) Thus in spite of the fact that throughout the entire Vietnam War the media had labored to create the fear that the mining of Haiphong harbor and the bombing of Hanoi's industrial and military installations would cause general war, it did not occur.†

Before that fallacy was clearly exposed as fraudulent, however, more than 360,000 Americans had been killed or wounded or had died from disease or accidents. And more than five million South and North Vietnamese battle casualties had occurred, in addition to countless civilian dead and injured.

What the news media in the United States had been saying, in effect, was that the Russian and Chinese Communists would not make it a general war, so long as we simply continued piling up casualties on both sides but made no attempt to win. But the mo-

---

*A Soldier Reports, by General William C. Westmoreland is indispensable to a full understanding of the Vietnam War.

† While President Nixon was in Moscow on this visit Mr. Brezhnev angrily denounced him, in a face-to-face meeting, for the bombing. The Soviet leader was said to have been in a towering, livid rage. It was not reported at the time. Yet the Soviet Government made no threats of war.

ment we began to seek victory, the Soviets and Chinese would enter the conflict and make it a wide-open war. Actually, the United States as well as South and North Vietnam were being bled. The lesson was clear: Wars must be fought to quick victory or not at all. The East Europeans, who know the Soviet Reds best, feel that there was never any likelihood that they would take on the United States in a war over Indochina. It is far more likely that the Soviet manipulators viewed the Vietnam War strictly as an enervating operation. They knew that the United States would never seek a clearcut victory. They sought, therefore, to prolong the conflict for its great nuisance effect in America and around the world. In this Moscow had success aplenty.

On April 30, 1975, the Vietnam War came to a formal end with the surrender of the Government of South Vietnam in Saigon to the Communist invaders. The last Americans were taken out of Saigon by helicopter. "This action closes a chapter in the American experience," said President Gerald Ford. After the American Civil War, it was the sorriest chapter. It was another in the series of defeats inflicted upon the free world by the Communists since the end of World War II.

Accuracy in Media, Inc., in its AIM/REPORT of April 1975 published an excellent analysis of "How the Media Helped Defeat Us" and the method used in "Covering Up The Consequences." But the media did not do it alone. The many and nefarious ways in which the United States Department of Defense under Secretary McNamara positively prevented America from winning the war are hardly touched upon here. And these actions caused many thousands of Americans and their allies to die or be wounded on the battlefields of Indo-China.

We know now that the no-victory principles stated by Walt Whitman Rostow during the Kennedy Administration were in fact set forth even more specifically in National Security Council document number 68 (NSC-68). That instrument, signed by President Truman on April 12, 1950, was classified and kept secret for twenty-five years. In 1975 it was declassified so quietly that the public, even the cognoscenti, were unaware of it.

Alice Widener devoted the September 3, 1976 issue of her

magazine, *U.S.A.*, to NSC-68. From that publication, we learned the truth about the imposition of the no-victory principle upon the United States. NSC-68 almost certainly brought on the Korean War, for it assured the Soviet Government that it need not fear defeat. It was in that document that Secretary of State Dean Acheson put Korea outside the line that the United States was prepared to defend in the Pacific. It strains credulity to suppose that the Russians were not immediately informed of the contents of NSC-68. Mrs. Widener describes its purposes as follows:

> Despite complete recognition of the stark reality of the Soviet threat to our country, both military and ideological, the principal aims of NSC-68 are:
>
> 1.—to avoid nuclear war but to accept a Soviet nuclear first strike against us if necessary, hoping to ward it off by building up our own and our allies' military, economic and social strength as a "deterrent";
> 2.—to confine U.S. military actions to strictly limited counteractions;
> 3.—to seek "coexistence" with the Soviet Union in the hope that democracy would win out eventually against dictatorship, that time would be on our side, and that the USSR would undergo changes eventually leading to abandonment of its goal of world domination;
> 4.—to try to "contain" the expansion of the Soviet Union beyond its own territory, but not to do anything "directly challenging Soviet prestige."

Almost all of NSC-68 is based on the analysis and policies advocated in George F. Kennan's 8,000-word paper, "The Sources of Soviet Conduct," first drafted by Kennan in 1945 while he was chargé d'affaires at the U.S. Embassy in Moscow with Ambassador Averell Harriman.

The National Security Council document itself, on page 6, described the aims of the Soviet leaders and world Communism:

> The fundamental design of those who control the Soviet Union and the international communist movement is to retain and solidify

their absolute power, first in the Soviet Union and second in the areas now under their control. In the minds of the Soviet leaders, however, achievement of this design requires the dynamic extension of their authority and the ultimate elimination of any effective opposition to their authority.

The design, therefore, calls for the complete subversion or forcible destruction of the machinery of government and structure of society in the countries of the non-Soviet world and their replacement by an apparatus and structure subservient to and controlled from the Kremlin. To that end Soviet efforts are now directed toward domination of the Eurasian land mass. The United States, as the principal center of power in the non-Soviet world and the bulwark of opposition to Soviet expansion, is the principal enemy whose integrity and vitality must be subverted or destroyed by one means or another if the Kremlin is to achieve its fundamental design.

Mrs. Widener comments with unconcealed bitterness:

> NSC-68 determined and evidently still determines American foreign policy and military strategy. The philosophy of NSC-68 became so pervasive that it constituted the way of thinking of the U.S. Government no matter who was President, Secretary of State and Secretary of Defense. The philosophy of NSC-68 still is all-pervasive in U.S. foreign policy.
>
> Every American has a right to know what is in NSC-68. It is the key to the lock of the secret box containing all the answers to all the agonized questions asked about our no-win military strategy and overall foreign policy by so many Americans, both prominent and plain citizens.

Not only are the policies of NSC-68 in effect today; they were also in effect between 1945 and April 12, 1950, when they became the official principles of the United States Government in diplomatic and military affairs. It is these principles and policies that have caused the great loss of American, allied, and enemy lives in two great wars, and has stultified American behavior in many other ways.

CHAPTER 7

Revolt Against War Without Patriotism

JEFFREY HART, PROFESSOR at Dartmouth College, Yale Ph.D., and author of a newspaper column for King Features Syndicate, made a memorable contribution to understanding in the spring of 1973. He observed that the United States had, "in effect," two goverments. There was the regular government elected by the people, and there was "a kind of counter-government."

The counter-government did not recognize the legality of the regular government, but on the contrary used every means, "legal and illegal," to counteract its policies. Mr. Hart noted that the counter-government assumed the right to declassify secret documents, as was done by Daniel Ellsberg, and that Tom Wicker, left-wing columnist, viewed Ellsberg and his colleague, Anthony J. Russo, Jr., as heroes.

Mr. Hart added that the counter-government within the official government steadily leaked information of all kinds to the press. For instance, Mr. Hart remarked, Dr. Kissinger could advise President Nixon of some sensitive foreign policy situation one day and read about it the next morning in Jack Anderson's column.

He pointed out that the counter-government had its own journalists, its own clergy (Groppi, the Berrigans, *et al.*), and its own lawyers (Ramsey Clark, Leonard Boudin, and William Kunstler among others). He noted that the counter-government was linked with the counter-culture, and that the counter-culture rejected the usual standards of "American behavior and style."

Mr. Hart stated his own feeling that the McGovern "movement" represented the highest point of the counter-culture and the counter-government, so that it was not without reason that "the

Watergate operatives perceived the McGovernites as alien and hostile, as enemies.''

Since Ellsberg looked upon the regular government as 'criminal,'' Mr. Hart said, and was lionized for his attitude and actions, the Liddys and McCords were bound to be "just around the corner.''

Taking a reasonable view of the thousands of youths who did not want to give their lives in a war that the United States government would not allow its military to win does not mean that the writer of this book condones draft-dodging, or looks with indifference upon the great deviations that the "counter-culture" produced. Indeed, the many instances of treasonous activities in America were sad to witness, and horrible to contemplate. Yet many thoughtful and patriotic youths across the country confided in this writer that they were not happy with the prospect of fighting in a no-win Indochina conflict in which our Government took an almost frivolous attitude toward the loss of life — squandering the lives of Americans and their allies by the hundreds of thousands.

One veteran of World War I claimed that today's youth were "afraid to face the bullet.'' But he failed to consider that young Americans were being told to offer themselves as targets in a war which the newspapers and other communications media condemned as unnecessary and wrong. Thus, the psychological base that had been provided for Americans fighting in every other war, including Korea, was pulled from under the young men and their officers in Indochina. The government was also divided with regard to support for our soldiers — to such an extent that targets chosen by the Chiefs of Staff for aerial attack in North Vietnam were in many cases rejected by Robert S. McNamara when he was Defense Secretary.

Even so, millions of Americans who either volunteered or were drafted did serve in Indochina. They fought against a foe as ruthless as had ever faced the American military. And they were as brave and competent as their fathers in previous wars — even without the great moral support of a united country. The divisive elements that were tearing the country apart at home caused repercussions in Vietnam. These young men in a strange land were sub-

91

jected to every conceivable pressure to defect, to become drug addicts, to mutiny, to fight each other in color conflicts, and to engage in other disputes of various kinds. The press magnified these problems, but they did exist. It failed to discuss at all the manner in which the war was fought, and this failure made inevitable many unnecessary casualties among soldiers and civilians alike.

Men serving in the ranks in other wars could turn to their officers — commissioned and noncommissioned — for a sensible explanation of what was going on. No such explanation could be given in Vietnam, for even the highest-ranking officers in Washington were kept in the dark about underlying policies. For the first time in American history the United States Armed Forces were treated as the enemy by the leading newspaper in the nation *The New York Times*, which kept up its attack even after President Nixon had withdrawn all American fighting men from South Vietnam. In its insidious attacks, the *Times* had the collaboration of many other newspapers, radio stations, and television networks. By their participation they gave either positive or tacit backing to the balance-of-power policy designed to hold the United States in check while the Communist world was being built up for an eventual world coalition government.

The "freedom marches" began in the southern states in 1961 the first year in which American casualties were recorded in Vietnam. As the war continued and American casualties mounted, the widest disequilibration in the lives of American youths and young adults in the history of the republic took place. The connection was obvious. Most human beings are at their best during their youth and young manhood. Their greatest ideas are hatched or conceived in that period. The youthful human mind is a delicate, complicated, and highly explosive mechanism. It reflects the problems the machinations, the hidden contretemps of the times. It reacts in mysterious ways. Some thousands of youths fled from this country to Canada and other lands.* (A *New York Times* reporter se

---

* The Canadian Consulate in New York would say only that in recent years about 25,000 Americans (of all ages) had migrated annually to Canada to settle there From the office of the Assistant United States Secretary of Defense, Lieutena

REVOLT AGAINST WAR WITHOUT PATRIOTISM

0,000 as a conservative estimate of the number who fled.) About 35 deserted from the Armed Forces and took refuge in Sweden — a nation noted for its vicious denunciations of the United States over the Vietnam War, though its own contributions to maintaining the freedom of the West have not been notable.

The nonconformity of American youth in this unparalleled situation gave rise to a whole new set of customs — mustachios, fuzzy sideburns, beards, and long flowing hair, making it difficult at times from the rear view to distinguish young men from young women. Many girls participated in the new dress styles by wearing blue jeans or Levis identical to the men's, long flowing hair, and no makeup. And the girls joined in many rebellious activities carried on by the young men. Ché Guevara, an Argentine revolutionary who helped to take over Cuba for the Communists and afterward was slain in Bolivia, became the model for many young Americans, so that it was possible on certain streets of New York City to see as many as three Ché Guevaras in one block. The real Ché Guevara and his leader Fidel Castro were early admirers of Hitler.

Hippiedom, offshoot of the basic nonconformism and revolt against the no-victory war, spawned a hundred thousand full-time, non-working drug users and about one million part-time, or "plastic," hippies. They spurned Christianity, serious thought, or any kind of sensible ethics toward their environment or one another. The young men often induced the young women to become prostitutes to provide "bread" for the commune. Although in the main they were not Communists, they could be — and were — used by the leftists because of their great vulnerability. The hippies represent an extreme descent into know-nothingism and do-nothingism, stemming from the impact of the Atomic Age with its vast dangers and from the unaccustomed behavior of the United States in refusing to win victories while offering up its sons to what in the 1960's appeared to be an endless war. Suzanne Labin in her perceptive and engaging work, *Hippies, Drugs and Pro-*

Colonel Audrey E. Thomas, United States Air Force, informed the writer that, as of December 7, 1972, "approximately 1,600 U.S. military personnel administratively classified as deserters are listed as being in Canada."

miscuity, called hippies "worshippers at the altar of indolence."*

Essentially this is the area which has been most debased in bleeding America — scores of thousands of youths debauched an unable to cope with national and international maladjustments They too are casualties. Many of them have died from overdoses o drugs or as beggars in faraway lands — Afghanistan, India, Nepal Hippiedom is an ugly pustulation on the face of America and th world. It is not an obvious threat to the nation because the hippie are aimless, mindless, feckless, and filled with a death wish; bu neither is it a credit or a help to the country. And insofar as the hip pies do not assist America, they hurt it.

While sometimes lawless, these young rebels do not have record of wide-spread violence and bloodshed. Theirs was wistful, introverted revolt. Not so the rebellions and insurrection of college students and Negroes. ("Blacks" is the word preferre by the left wing for designating Negroes. "Colored people" is descriptive term greatly derided by the Leftists, though the Na tional Association for the Advancement of Colored People has n changed its name. Polls taken among Negroes revealed that the did not prefer "blacks" but would accept "Negroes" or "colore people" where a designation was felt to be necessary at a "Blacks" is a polarizing word with invidious possibilities; it precisely the kind of designation that is designed to widen th separation of the peoples. The idea of two distinct *races* of man repugnant to reason and is without scientific basis.) Color whether black, brown, yellowish or tan — was the basis for th enslavement of and discrimination against Negroes. After the pe formances of Stalin and Hitler in this century, nobody can clai rationally that white leadership alone is a guarantee against th establishment of brutal and murderous tyrannies, unparallel since the days of Genghis Khan in the thirteenth century.

The decade of 1961-1970 saw the greatest number of riots a instances of violence, looting, burning, and seizure of buildings the history of the United States. Insurrectionary behavior on t part of some Negroes preceded upheavals by students in colleg

* *Hippies, Drugs and Promiscuity,* by Suzanne Labin, page 46.

94

across the country. Eugene H. Methvin summed up the situation and its causes brilliantly in his work *The Riot Makers.* He recalled that in the summer of 1964 Harlem had erupted in a blazing riot, and that similar outbreaks followed in six other cities. Within ten days after the murder of Dr. Martin Luther King in 1968 fiery riots had occurred in 125 cities. Methvin saw a number of possible causes for the disorders, but he concluded that they "came about because there were those who wanted them to come about" and "did everything in their power to cause them."

Of the 11,261 persons arrested in riots in Watts (Los Angeles), Newark, Detroit, and Toledo, 56 percent had previously served jail sentences of ninety days or more. Which is to say that the criminal element had been enlisted in the events that were made to happen. "You gotta stop looting and start shooting!" counseled H. Rap Brown, chairman of the Student Nonviolent Coordinating Committee (SNCC), which might better have been called the Non-Student Violent Coordinating Committee. "We have to move from Molotov cocktails to dynamite," Stokely Carmichael told a group in Harlem. In 1967 Carmichael advised an audience in Cincinnati, as the police stood by, to "stop fighting each other and go out and fight the police." Methvin concluded that a "generation of radicals has adopted the Leninist methodology of planned violence."

The long smoldering discontent of Negroes and the readiness of lawless persons among them to join in violent action were the tinder utilized by the Communist "movement" to ignite havoc in every part of the country. Links to the Communists were everywhere in evidence. Blatantly, the leaders visited Havana, where Castro provided schools for guerrillas in urban warfare and national revolution.

It is not the function of this work to ascertain all the underlying and latent causes of the riots, or to tabulate the total losses in lives and property — a total that may *never* be accurately computed. The greatest injury to America was in the undermining of her foreign and domestic policies and the division of a distraught nation. America offered a spectacle of helplessness to a world badly in need of her leadership and support, so that some Europeans began speaking of the United States as "the muscle-bound giant."

95

Sicco Mansholt of the Common Market predicted that this country was already so far down the drain that nothing could save it, and was not qualified to be the leader of the world anyhow — a view, of course, which this writer does not share in any way and which he feels to be thoroughly unmerited in light of the vast contributions that the United States has made to the world, contributions unmatched by any other nation in all history. But the Communists and their allies in misery might have been expected to do all in their power to distract and obstruct Americans in the benevolent work of fostering freedom around the world. They are attempting to do just that by weakening her prestige abroad and her stability at home.

Dr. Albert Einstein once said that "only strong characters can resist the temptation of superficial analysis." The writer hopes that the brevity of this chapter will not expose him to the charge of having succumbed to that temptation, for he believes the matters discussed here are of crucial importance. He therefore counsels the reader to go to Methvin's *The Riot Makers* for a more complete and a profoundly interesting study of this great upheaval in American life. It is important that we learn everything possible about this phenomenal period, for it is an important page in our history. Americans must know and understand what has happened to their civilization and culture.

The demolition artists are burrowing deeper and deeper into American public and private life. They do not harangue the people about life, liberty, and the pursuit of happiness; they do not extol the "correctness" of trial by jury and of courts beyond the reach of corruption; they don't harp on personal probity and the ennoblement of working, of owning a home, of sustaining religion as a fundamental freedom, of upholding freedom of enterprise as a cardinal tenet of liberty; they don't explain the importance of opposing government operation of business, the constant expansion of taxes to meet the costs of newly devised social programs, the ever rising deficits in domestic budgets, the unfavorable foreign balances. The demolitionists are more concerned about constantly expanding welfare budgets and government handouts of all kinds. Above all, they are working to gain total ascendancy over the American government. From this base, they would proceed to stifle the liberties, the guarantees, the prosperity, and the hopes that now exist for an orderly world.

The revolt of American students was one of the most extraordinary occurrences in our history. Its effects are still being felt, even though its fury is dying, if not already dead. At its apex it resulted in the seizure and destruction of buildings on university campuses throughout the nation. Eight students — four at Kent State in Ohio, two at Jackson State in Mississippi, and two at Southern University in Louisiana — were killed. A graduate student, the father of three small children, was killed at the University of Wisconsin when a bomb placed by revolutionaries exploded. Three young persons were arrested in connection with a bank holdup in Washington, D.C., in which a policeman was slain. The young couple involved were planning to set up a "commune" in Virginia. A number of persons, including a policeman, were grievously wounded in a riot at Columbia University in New York City. A bank building at the University of California at Santa Barbara was burned to the ground.

CHAPTER 8

Death Of
The Monroe Doctrine

It was censored last week by CBS, but [former President] Lyndon Johnson has severe doubts about the Warren Commission he himself set up. Johnson told CBS interviewers — in the deleted portion [of the censored interview] that the commission made a major error in ruling out a Communist conspiracy [in the assassination of President Kennedy]. Johnson expressed serious reservations about the "motivations and connections" of Lee Harvey Oswald, specifically his ties to the Soviet Union, Communist Cuba and the Fair Play for Cuba Committee.

— *Human Events*, May 9, 1970

The world is governed by different personages from what is imagined by those who are not behind the scenes.

— Benjamin Disraeli

THE FALL OF CUBA to the Communists, which was set up during the administration of Dwight D. Eisenhower,* brought about the death of the Monroe Doctrine. It is comprehensible only as a deliberate action of the United States Government. No one can assume that the United States did not have the power to prevent this critical loss to the security of the entire hemisphere. Nor can

---

* See *The Politician*, by Robert Welch (Belmont, Massachusetts: Belmont Publishing Company, 1964).

anyone believe that the United States Government did not know the background of Fidel Castro and the Soviet forces behind him.

As a reminder of the essence of the Monroe Doctrine, we quote from the *International Encyclopedia:*

> [Monroe Doctrine is] the term applied to the policy of the United States regarding foreign interference in American affairs. It takes its name from President Monroe, who in his message to Congress in 1823 first gave it formal announcement . . . . In modern conception it is the policy of the United States to regard any attempt on the part of a European power to gain a foothold in this hemisphere by conquest, or to acquire any new establishment in North or South America by whatever means, as an act hostile to the United States.

Through the installation of a Communist regime in Cuba, the Soviet Government achieved a military and political stronghold in the American hemisphere. Premier Nikita Khrushchev declared that the Monroe Doctrine was dead — for he had killed it. The Russians are well aware that they are the beneficiaries of American appeasement. Their real problem is to determine the limit to which they can expand.

The national news media are evidently unconcerned as to whether the American people learn the truth about Russia's rising strength. This unconcern was evidenced once again in August 1971, when News Perspective International, headed by William J. Gill, reported to its customers from Washington:

> Two nights before Congress adjourned for its summer recess eighty-six members of the House of Representatives joined in issuing one of the most ominous warnings in the history of the republic.
>
> One by one, Congressmen from both parties rose on the floor of the House and laid it on the line: If the United States continues to fall behind the Soviet Union in nuclear, naval and all other armaments, the survival of the nation — and the lives of every man, woman and child in the country — will soon be in jeopardy.
>
> In short, America will cease to exist.
>
> Yet not one national television news show featured this story: not a line of it appeared in *The New York Times* nor the *Washington Post,* and so far as the Congressmen could immediately determine neither the Associated Press nor United Press International carried it

on their national wires.

The national news media decided these Congressmen have no right to be heard. As one disgusted House member from Illinois put it, "If Bella Abzug had dropped her bra on the Capitol steps it would have hit every TV screen and every front page in the country. But we get blanked completely on something like this."

The question that must be posed at this point is this: Why have the news media imposed a virtual Iron Curtain of Censorship on this, the most important story of our time?

One may question whether this was the most important story of our time. One may criticize the anxiety of the eighty-six members of the House of Representatives over the growing strength of the Soviet Union. But there can be no question about the right of the public to know what these Members of the House were saying, and there can be no denying the duty of the news media to present their views to the people.

Documentation concerning involvement of the United States Government in a long-range plot to wreck the non-Communist government of Cuba and hand it over to the Communists has been outlined in a number of works published since World War II. In one recent opus, *The Experts*, published in 1968, the authors, Seymour Freidin and George Bailey, remarked (page 135) that "the Communist conspiracy that flourished [in the United States Government] during the late thirties and early forties was largely obscured and has remained so."

Freidin and Bailey contended that Harry Dexter White was the most important member of that conspiracy, "because he was the most effective agent of the Soviet Union." They said that he had been recruited by the OGPU, later the KGB (Soviet Secret Police), in the early 1920's while he was a student at Stanford University. He "was not an agent of influence, but a regularly recruited, trained Soviet agent who was groomed and managed by his Soviet case officers for his career." White rose during the 1930's to become Assistant Secretary of the Treasury of the United States, and he brought into the department "his fellow Communists in such numbers and into such positions as to make the Treasury Department and most of its branches a Communist stronghold in

American government." Freidin and Bailey also observed that because of White's great influence at policy-making levels he was able to effect "far-reaching changes in our government."

Indeed, it has been asserted that White was responsible for the transfer to the Soviets of the plates and other equipment for printing German occupation marks at the end of World War II. That transfer cost the United States more than 200 million dollars before Washington put a stop to the bleeding operation. White was also "credited" with having engineered the runaway inflation of the Chinese yuan, a maneuver that helped to bring on economic chaos and the collapse of the Government of Chiang Kai-shek on the Chinese mainland. And the hand of Harry Dexter White was seen in the Italian peace treaty, which gave $360 million in reparations to Soviet Russia, Yugoslavia, Greece, Ethiopia, and Albania, "all billed to the American taxpayers since the war left Italy destitute." In addition, the Russians received nearly half of the Italian merchant marine and more than half of the Italian Navy.

Far from being discredited immediately, after he left the Treasury Department White was appointed United States representative on the executive board of the World Bank. He died suddenly in 1946 after testifying before a committee of the House of Representatives.

The interlocking nature of the Communist apparatus in the United States Government and Harry Dexter White's consistently destructive activities in behalf of Communists around the world are detailed further in *Diplomats and Demagogues: The Memoirs of Spruille Braden*. Mr. Braden was one of the ablest American diplomats in Latin America. He said in his book that as United States Ambassador to Cuba in the early 1940's, the first thing he did in Cuba was "to defeat a Communist plot involving both our State and Treasury Departments." He stated that Harry Dexter White had visited Cuba where he had recommended that the island country should have its own currency and a central bank with a series of subsidiary banks. The United States envoy said he immediately foresaw the possibility of galloping inflation, which would undoubtedly have been followed by economic chaos. This is, of course, the Communist formula for conquest. For his pains in saving Cuba from fiscal ruin Mr. Braden was attacked in a message from the State Department which said that "Cuba had a sovereign right to its own bank and currency" and that he "was apparently a tool of the American banking interests in Cuba." Mr. Braden observed that this "was a few years before Harry Dexter White, who ran Secretary Morgenthau, and Lawrence Duggan, who ran our Latin American relations, were exposed as members of the Soviet spy apparatus."

This insidious endeavor to debase the currency of Cuba was scotched, though the attempt in China succeeded. The Communists win some, and they lose some. But they never stop trying. In Cuba they succeeded the second time around, by a new route, but once again with yeoman assistance from the United States Government. Obviously the United States currency itself is now under the most violent and sustained attack in its history. Why is it that the currency of the richest country in the world is so weak, and is being buffeted in the world's financial capitals? We know the technical answers. But do we know why the vast deficits in our accounts at home and abroad were rolled up in the first place? If this is not the work of a conspiracy, how has it been done?

The weakening of the United States has continued unabated since the end of World War II. While the course may zig and zag, it is not marked by any great victories. Indeed, a victory would soon be counted as a defeat. And the manipulators of our fate would simply work for a new defeat to undo or downgrade anything that might be construed as a win. On the other hand, it is interesting to note the number of Communist agents who, individually, come to disastrous ends. For example, Spruille Braden recounted that on December 29, 1947, "Duggan jumped, or he was thrown, from the window of his office in midtown Manhattan."

Braden provided us with some inside glimpses of the State Department in Washington that indicated the strength of Communist penetration in that and other departments. He told of an FBI report, circulated among top officials, that identified as Communists a number of government employees, including Harry Dexter White and Alger Hiss. Braden also said that, in spite of many efforts, he was never able to get "any real discussion of the Communist peril while in the State Department." Memos on this matter were met "with evasion," he said, and he constantly had the feeling of someone "shut up in a dark room vainly trying to catch a black cat." Yet, he recalled, things happened that he found hard to explain except as the work of "a communist hand acting in the shadows."

Braden described how dispatches from the United States Embassy in Argentina to Washington, and a memorandum sent to Washington by an Argentine Ambassador in Uruguay, found their way into Peron's newspaper in Buenos Aires. This happened during a period of cooperation between Communists and Peronists. He felt it was not likely the Peronists had infiltrated the State Department, but thought the Communists had; and it was probable that they had photostated the letters and sent them to Argentina. Also, a long memorandum on Communism that Ambassador Braden sent from Cuba disappeared from the files of both the State Department in Washington and the U.S. Embassy in Havana. Eight hundred documents containing the names, aliases, and addresses of Communist agents all over the American hemisphere also disappeared from the State Department. They had been photostated in Rio de Janeiro by U.S. Ambassador Hugh Gibson and sent to Washington.

Eight hundred documents listing the names and addresses of Communist agents all over the hemisphere simply vanished!

But the State Department somehow always manages to escape a house-cleaning. In 1952 the people turned out the Democrats and voted in General Dwight D. Eisenhower partly because of "popular concern over the Communist infiltration of the State Department that had been exposed by Congressional investigations and the two Hiss trials." But the new Secretary of State, John Foster Dulles, "rushed around the world at such a pace that the hoped-for purge of Communists never took place." We cannot accept Mr. Braden's explanation for the failure — for the promised purge never *does* take place. Eight years later Richard M. Nixon, during his first run for the Presidency, said in Dallas, Texas, that if he were elected he would undertake a complete housecleaning of the State Department. But when Nixon was finally elected, in 1968, exactly the opposite is reported to have happened; that is, a purge of pro- Nixon people in the department was said to be under way soon after Mr. Nixon entered the White House in 1969. At any rate, there was no purge of the State Department by President Nixon. He said things looked different from inside the White House — an ominous statement that has never been explained or amplified.

The Braden memoirs throw much light upon the activities of Alger Hiss in the State Department and the apparently close connection between Hiss and others in State Department work. The efforts of Hiss in 1946 to deprive the United States of sovereignty over the Panama Canal Zone is also detailed by Spruille Braden, who at that time was Assistant Secretary of State for Latin American affairs.

This writer's long-standing distrust of Dean Acheson was not diminished by reading Braden's *Memoirs.* Braden made it clear that he never expected to find Acheson on his side in any difference with Hiss. In fact, after Hiss was accused of perfidy, Acheson announced publicly that he would not turn his back on Alger Hiss.* Why was it more important to defend Hiss than to reveal the truth about him? Why did Braden find it impossible to discuss the Communist peril while in the State Department? Why did he have the feeling of being shut up "in a dark room vainly trying to catch a black cat"? Acheson and Braden were both Yale graduates, but they were worlds apart in their thinking. It was Braden who was forced out of the State Department. Why? He was one of the ablest and most rigidly loyal men in the State Department. Was he pressured into leaving because he would not ride the left-wing "wave of the future"? Braden, of course, refused to lend himself to a policy of confusing the American people. That was his undoing.

Since the days of Braden and Acheson, security has been completely smashed in the State Department, and the public has not the faintest idea what kind of thinking is to be found there. Further,

---

* Note how different was the behavior of Chancellor Willy Brandt of West Germany in 1974 when his top aide, Gunther Guillaume, was exposed as an East German spy in the West German government. Herr Brandt did not say, "I will not turn my back on Gunther Guillaume." On the contrary, Herr Brandt resigned.

the problems facing America on the international scene were exacerbated by Dr. Henry A. Kissinger, who, during the first Nixon Administration, undertook most of the negotiations in foreign affairs, while the role of the Secretary of State was cast into the shadows. At the same time, the United States State Department was deliberately deprived of any security by the removal of Otto Otepka and other security experts.

Let us now briefly scan two important subjects — the right of the United States to be in the Panama Canal zone, and the fall of Cuba to the Communists.

The United States is now negotiating a new treaty with the government of Panama regarding the Canal. And a special Presidential commission has recommended that the United States build a new, sea-level canal across the isthmus of Panama, just west of the present non-sea-level canal. This proposed new canal is being used as a pretext for yielding sovereignty over the present Canal Zone. It would duplicate the existing facility at an initial cost of nearly $3 billion. The sea-level job would be a vast boondoggle that would waste the taxpayers' money, introduce vast ecological hazards, and possibly result in a new Suez Canal situation — that is, a complete shutdown of one of the world's vital waterways. Such a disaster could occur if either of the proposed new treaties were ratified. The present canal has the ability to handle future increases in traffic through improvements already proposed in Congress — improvements that could be accomplished at a small fraction of the cost of an unnecessary new sea-level canal.

Many members of Congress were greatly concerned in both 1972 and 1974 when the United States Government revealed plans for ceding its sovereignty and jurisdiction over the Canal Zone to Panama, a country dominated by what Professor Donald M. Dozer has called the "saber-rattling demagogy of Brig. General Omar Torrijos, Supreme Leader of the Revolutionary Government of Panama."* Communists in the Panamanian government, aided by the Soviets, had already instigated trouble and disorders in Panama. Although these subversive efforts were reported from

---

* *Human Events*, November 4, 1972, page 12.

many sources, none of the reports emanated from the United States Government or appeared in the major American news media.

Three United States ambassadors — Robert B. Anderson, John C. Mundt, and David H. Ward — for more than a year have been negotiating new treaties with Panama concerning the Canal Zone. As in virtually all such negotiations with Leftists, none of the rights of Torrijos' brutal dictatorship are under negotiation; only the rights of the United States are being dealt away. For Communists always negotiate on the basis that "What's mine is mine; only what's yours is negotiable."

From 1904 through June 30, 1971, the United States had put, including defense, $5,695,745,000 into the canal. Every bit of the land in the Canal Zone had been purchased, parcel by parcel, from the owners. The territory was granted to the United States — not leased — in perpetuity in consideration of a cash payment to the Panama Government of $10 million and agreement to pay an annual sum of $250,000 to compensate for Panama's loss of revenue from the Panama Railroad. By 1955 the latter figure had been increased to $1.9 million. This was never a rental payment. Shortly after Panama declared its independence from Colombia, the Hay —Bunau-Varilla Treaty with the United States was signed.

Robert Morris, an eminent constitutional lawyer, contributed a remarkable editorial to the Catholic weekly *Twin Circle* of March 22, 1974, which is so corroborative of the position described in this work that it is reproduced here in entirety:

> Perspective is so important. It enables one to see clearly. That is why the sly but successful propagandists are always throwing dust in our eyes.
>
> For seemingly inexplicable reasons the U.S. State Department has been trying to take the Panama Canal from the United States and turn it over to the Panamanian Government which is run by political bandits allied to Fidel Castro and Colonel Qaddafi and other enemies of the United States.
>
> They have no legal authority to do so since sovereignty over the canal was formally ceded to the United States in perpetuity in 1903. The ceding was wrought by treaty which under our Constitution becomes the law of the land, equal to the Constitution.

Death Of The Monroe Doctrine

No President, much less the State Department, has the power or authority to change this deeply ingrained constitutional enactment by executive agreement.

To amend or to annul this treaty, which is what Dr. Henry Kissinger, through Ambassador Ellsworth Bunker, is trying to do, legislative action must be taken by a two-thirds vote in the House of Representatives.

But Kissinger and Bunker are acting as if they and not the Congress have the authority to take this step which a clear perspective would show to be suicidal and self-destructive.

If Panamanian dictator Torrijos is given sovereignty and authority over the Canal, he and his allies will see to it that we will not use the Canal at all or else we will be blackmailed into outrageous payments and conditions. That is the booming lesson of contemporary history. To try to safeguard our interest by agreement after surrendering sovereignty is fanciful.

All of which points up the folly of our present policy of détente. The Communists and their allies (of which Torrijos is one) are driving ahead toward their goal of Sovietizing the world. We are peacefully and unilaterally co-existing with them, even to the extent of foregoing any educational implementation of our posture.

We sent troops into Vietnam to stem the Communists but we could not indoctrinate them that Communism was an evil force of aggression. When soldiers know not for what they fight, they lose their morale. And when parents know not for what their sons fight and die, they do more than lose morale.

How can we survive in a world with aggressive Soviet power when all our agencies of government are precluded, by authority on high, to educate our people on the true nature of Communism?

Every Soviet bureaucrat is imbued with a sense of dedication to Communist advancement. Every bureaucrat of ours must be neutral to Communism (or worse) to be eligible for service.

It necessarily follows that our present policy will take us into one retreat after another. The enemy can implement its aggressions with propaganda and demonstrations. We can only implement our position with abstract, often inane and now thoroughly incredible protests and pretensions.

Let there be thorough hearings in the Senate and even the House of Representatives on the issue of the Panama Canal. Then let the Congress make its decision. Let us not engage in the secret diplomacy that has led us into one disaster after another.

Unfortunately, it is only rarely that so logical a position in regard to American policy is heard in the land.

The fall of Cuba to the Communists in January 1959 removed from this writer's mind any lingering doubts that the United States was in serious danger at home and abroad from Communist machinations. True, hindsight generally has 20-20 vision. But this is a sight better than none! Some among us do not even have hindsight. Some are Communists. A great smoke screen about *McCarthyites, reactionaries*, and *imperialists* was thrown up to cover the assistance of the United States Government in putting the Castro regime in power. When the massive Cuban massacres (more than 20,000 executions of innocent persons in a few years) left some gnawing doubts about the Frankenstein that had been created for the Americas,* a new mind-clouding device was developed. The term "anti-Communist" was made disreputable — that is, only a vulgar, uneducated boor would be an anti-Communist. It was not proper even to express concern about the seizures by the Cuban Communists of about three billion dollars' worth of property of American citizens. *The New York Times* was most vociferous in helping to bring Castro to power and to keep him there at all costs. It had yeoman help from other newspapers and from the electronic media. But above all it had the help of the United States Government — help that was essential in bringing the Communists to power and in killing the Monroe Doctrine. It would be dangerously naïve to assume that the individuals within the United States Government who worked so hard for Mr. Castro and his comrades were either stupid or incompetent.

Sources of information about Cuba are many and varied. Two outstanding works are Mario Lazo's *American Policy Failures in Cuba* (1970, Twin Circle edition) and Paul D. Bethel's *The Losers* (1969, Arlington House). Both were written by honest and courageous men, thoroughly familiar with Cuba. These men

---

* Clarence M. Mitchell, Jr., a member of the United States delegation to the United Nations, put the number of political prisoners in Cuba at 20,000 on November 13, 1975.

witnessed the events they describe. Dr. Lazo nearly lost his life in the brutal and merciless killings ordered by Castro and Guevara. ("More than twice as many people had been killed in a single year than during the seventeen years Batista had held power, and thousands had been imprisoned," wrote Lazo.) Guevara, popularly portrayed as a romantic revolutionary who stole from the rich to help the poor, was in fact a compulsive killer who exterminated Cuban peasants as readily as the "bourgeoisie."

The question always arises of why important Americans, influential newspapers, and prominent persons in the United States Government should want to lend aid to such scoundrels. As we have indicated previously, the overriding concern of these men and institutions is the driving of the United States into a position where it must form a "coalition world government" with the Soviets and other Communist nations.

Everything indicates that the Cuban "revolution" was a skillfully engineered operation, cold-bloodedly calculated to transfer power from the Batista regime (which was not perfect by any means) to a clique of blood-thirsty gangsters. It was essential to Communist plans that Batista be removed from power, since he had already agreed to a provision that would keep Cuba a republic.

Our national news media warmly embraced Castro and cast him in the role of deliverer of oppressed Cubans. Castro delivered, but not in the manner promised. There were no elections. His "coalition" soon dissolved and it was revealed that Castro's basic solution was Communism. Russians were officially invited in, and all dissident Cubans were invited to leave. About 800,000 did just that. Those were the dissidents who were not killed by firing squads following drumhead trials that were in reality no trials at all. The Russians said they were amazed at the ease with which they were permitted to penetrate Cuba.

Readers of this volume would be well advised to read at least the two volumes on Cuba mentioned here, Dr. Lazo's and Paul Bethel's. Bethel shows clearly that Cuba is now completely controlled by the Soviets. Dr. Lazo makes it painfully apparent that the Cubans never had a chance of regaining their freedom once Castro was in power. The Bay of Pigs was a disaster far greater than we thought, for it was this clumsy and tragic farce in 1961 that encouraged the Russians to put missiles in Cuba in 1962, and thus risk a nuclear war (if, indeed, that was what the great contretemps was about).

This book has dealt with the principles that are being applied and the practices being employed in weakening the United States in relationship to the Soviet Union and other Communist powers. One can agree with Gary Allen's statement about Communism — that it is run more from New York, Washington, Paris, and London than from Moscow and Peking — without doubting that Moscow and Peking are spreading violence and confusion throughout the Western world, including especially the United States. When we become cognizant of the principles (or lack of them, morally speaking) that guide our national and individual destinies, we are able to understand the strange events occurring around us. For instance, we learn that Moscow may have more of a hand in the internal workings of the United States than even the most anti-Communist American has ever charged. Communist infiltration of political parties, the news media, book and magazine publishing, the teaching profession, the arts, sciences, and other professions, is deliberate and may be more widespread than is imagined. Conversely, the most outspoken anti-Soviet speaker may well deserve a second look — he could be a subverter, and a master subverter at that.

J. Bernard Hutton, a former member of the central committee of the Czech Communist party, who served as foreign editor of the newspaper *Vechernyaya Moskva (Evening Moscow),* became disillusioned with the Communist system as he observed it in Russia. After residing in London during World War II, he returned to Prague. He left again following the Communist takeover in 1948. Again returning to live in England, he devoted his life to exposing the great fraud that is Communism. His latest work is *The Subverters,* published in the United States by Arlington House. This fascinating eye-opener reveals how the Russians and Chinese Communists are working to upset the West through murder, air hijacking, fueling the war in Northern Ireland, strikes, sabotage, kidnapping, the entrapment of soldiers through the use of women into becoming traitors, and other crimes. Though they generally combine their efforts, Moscow and Peking have their differences.

These differences involve whether to use civil disruption or gelignite to produce chaos in the Western world. Peking got the jump on Moscow in the matter of air piracy and terrorism. The Chinese Communists trained individuals in the techniques of attacking aircraft with machine guns and incendiary bombs, and smuggling plastic hand grenades through airport checks. Moscow followed suit and established its own schools for air terrorists. It cannot be denied that Soviet Russia and Communist China have their differences, but the differences are between themselves, and concern how most effectively to subvert and subjugate the western world.

The Subverters is a fascinating compendium of information. Its facts frequently are given in the form of stories about the lives of individual subverters. It tells of activities that are rarely presented in depth in the news media. It was never likely that this book would be reviewed in New York or Washington by any of the leading book review magazines. Nor will Mr. Hutton hear on television the familiar words, "will you welcome, please, Mr. J. Bernard Hutton, author of *The Subverters*." The major newspapers, like the television and radio networks, do what they can to drive book publishers to the left. Joined by the tax-exempt foundations, they endeavor, almost always successfully, to crush conservative and truthful writers.

CHAPTER 9

Ecology: Taking America To The Cleaners

A great power that does not control its own energy sources is bound to degenerate into a blustering impostor . . . . When all the rhetoric has been exhausted, a little elementary arithmetic comes through loud and clear with only two possibilities of bridging the energy gap for the next decades — coal and nuclear fuel. Not either, but both.

— Dr. Petr Beckmann
The Review Of The News, July 23, 1975

DDT is one of mankind's major triumphs. It has been the principal insecticide in the control of insect vectors [carriers] of yellow fever, typhus, elephantiasis, bubonic plague, cholera, dengue, sleeping sickness and dysentery.

— Dr. Walter Ebeling
quoted in *The Disaster Lobby*

If DDT is banned by the United States, I have wasted my life's work [developing a new strain of wheat that doubles food production per acre wherever it is grown]. I have dedicated myself to finding better methods of feeding the world's starving populations. Without DDT and other important agricultural chemicals, our goals are simply unattainable.

— Dr. Norman Borlaug
Nobel Prize Winner

Equipment and modifications required to meet Federal safety and emissions standards add more than $700 to the price of an average 1975 model car. For the model year that amounts to a cost of more than $5 billion, a very impressive amount of money. But the return on the investment is far less impressive.

— John Riccardo
Chairman of Chrysler Corporation

MANY EDUCATED AND PATRIOTIC Americans are members of conservationist organizations. These groups for the most part are dedicated to preserving flora and fauna in the wild state, to maintaining the surface land scenery in its original state, and to purifying the air in the cities and countryside. Sometimes, however, the executives of these associations go beyond the aims and desires of the members, and their actions are inimical to the best interests of the nation. This chapter is not a blanket indictment of all ecologists.

It is only those actions that are threats to America's orderly growth and progress that concern us here. Ecology, environmentalism, and symbiosis are matters that merit the concern of all citizens. But when their importance is distorted by overemphasis, they can disrupt the normal economic and political growth of the country. Without a doubt this distortion is designed to do just that. For the persons and institutions that have worked so hard to build up the Soviet Union and to undermine America's ability to defend herself are to be found in the forefront of the ecological movement.

Ecological extremists, sometimes known as "ecofreaks" or "econuts," believe that it is necessary to take America to the cleaners. Anyone conversant with American slang knows that to be "taken to the cleaners" is to be given a beating, or a fleecing, or both. The ecofreaks pretend to be dedicated literally to cleaning up the environment and protecting Americans and their posterity. What they are attempting to protect, however, is not human beings, but rather animals, plant life, and scenery. The slang meaning of the term is far more accurate.

When the American people become aware of what is being done to them in the name of ecology, it is not likely that they will

113

stand by mute and helpless. Indeed, from the surface mining of coal to the use of DDT and hexachlorophene; from the production of oil, electricity, and automobiles to fishing and trapping for furs; extreme environmentalists have succeeded in confusing the public to a degree that must have astonished even them. The effect of their labors was felt in 1973 when a Middle Eastern oil cartel, encouraged by the Soviets and the no-win foreign policies of the United States, brought this country to its knees with the first great oil boycott in history. Ecology, like the overstaying guest, began to exhibit glaring faults.

Surface mining of coal, also known as strip mining, is an extraordinary technological feat. If it does not reduce the number of miners needed, it at least helps to keep additional men from having to enter the pits in one of the hardest and most dangerous livelihoods. Yet in its June 25, 1975 issue, *The Review Of The News* reported that at a time of national economic recession, Congress had "passed a bill that could throw 50,000 men out of work and jack up utility rates for virtually every consumer in America." This was the Strip Mining Bill, which received a presidential veto that was upheld by a margin of only three votes in Congress. The bill was designed to regulate the surface mining of coal. *The Review* observed that, under cover of protecting the environment, the measure would in fact have greatly curbed the output of coal, a well-nigh inexhaustible source of much-needed energy for America. It reported the estimate of Carl E. Bagge, president of the National Coal Association, that the proposed law would have reduced the national output of coal by 25 percent. And this article pointed to the Department of the Interior statement that such a loss would force the country to import 1.3 million barrels more of Arab oil daily. *The Review Of The News* commented:

> The environmental drawbacks in surface mining have been blown all out of proportion by kooks and Marxists who want to ensure a permanent shortage of oil, gas, coal and any other source of energy needed to keep our free economy humming.

The same weekly news publication reported in August 1975 that government interference in the oil market was believed by experts to be depriving the country of at least two million barrels of petroleum a day.

Following the demise of *Look* magazine, Melvin J. Grayson, a former vice president of *Look,* and Thomas R. Shepard, Jr., who had been its publisher, wrote a book titled *The Disaster Lobby: Prophets of Ecological Doom and Other Absurdities* (Follett Publishing Co., Chicago). They identified "the disaster lobby" as the Wilderness Society, the National Audubon Society, the Sierra Club, Friends of the Earth, Trout Unlimited, Ralph Nader, and others. And *U.S. News & World Report* for June 9, 1975, noted that most of the large ecological groups, including the Sierra Club and the Wilderness Society, reported regular increases in membership and financial support. The authors of *The Disaster Lobby* made the following remarkable statement:

> For some reason, apparently the production of energy and energy materials seemed to infuriate many environmentalists more than any other activity of mankind. Although they opposed most kinds of progress, they reserved their best efforts for those projects connected with the generation of power. Oil fields, coal mines, gas pipelines, electric power plants, all were special targets of the Disaster Lobby. And the more severe the nation's power shortage became in the 1960's and 1970's, the greater were the pressures against the kind of expansion that might have relieved the shortage.*

Although the energy output of the United States was still hobbled in 1975, and the shrill attacks on the surface mining of coal continued, surface mining went on. Through this method coal that is near the land surface is scooped out by huge mechanical shovels. It is true that the earth thus stripped of its greenery is not a pretty sight. But the inside of a coal mine is hardly an improvement, and not only is it ugly but it is also subject to the accumulation of noxious and explosive gases that often cause fires, bringing injury or death to men working in the pits. These and other hazards (the disease called black lung, for example) are not present in surface

*Grayson and Shepard, *op. cit.,* page 105.

mining. Moreover, the stripped land can be restored to its original state of natural beauty, and this has been done routinely. The inside of a coal mine is never restored or beautified; yet there is no outcry from the environmental activists, nor do they agitate on behalf of the deep-mine workers.

Carl E. Bagge, National Coal Association president quoted earlier, asserted in 1971 that much of the land turned over in surface mining in eastern Kentucky and West Virginia had already been restored, and that the rest was in the process of restoration. He reported:

> The laws vary, but in most cases they require the land to be graded, revegetated, and that a specified high percentage of the vegetation survive for one or two growing seasons. . . . We would be happy to show an impartial reporter thousands of acres of land reclaimed so thoroughly that it is difficult to tell it was once mined for coal . . . .
>
> Electric utilities used 198 million tons of surface mined coal in 1970 to produce 28.2 percent of all electric power generated in the United States. To replace that much surface mine output with deep mine production would require three to four years, recruiting more workers in an industry already short of skilled miners, and an investment of $2.5 billion or more — not to mention abolishing the jobs of men now employed in surface mining, junking the equipment and abandoning coal reserves which cannot be mined except by surface methods.

National Coal Association figures for 1972 showed that more surface-mined land was being returned to agricultural or scenic usefulness each year than was being stripped. The Friends of the Earth claimed that those figures were irrelevant, which suggests that we must look beyond mere logic to discover the reasons for the actions of the environmental extremists. If the extremists were logical or consistent, an uproar concerning the appearance of certain areas in Arizona and the Bad Lands of North and South Dakota might be expected. Yet the contrary is the case; the Sierra Club wants to preserve Arizona and the Dakotas as they are. In brief, you can make an issue out of anything if you so desire, contradictions notwithstanding.

"Government regulations have nearly wrecked transportation, almost bankrupted utilities [and not always *almost*], wreaked havoc on the auto industry, crippled many smaller companies — and all in 'the consumer's interest.' " That apt description appeared in *Industrial Press Service,* a publication of the National Association of Manufacturers. Or (we might add) hadn't you noticed? Which is not merely a flippant question, for in the busy lives of so many of us, and in view of the omissions, distortions, and fabrications of the national news media, it is quite possible for a great industry to be wrecked before the public becomes fully aware that it is happening, and how. Moreover, in the world-wide struggle that is now under way, it is frequently most difficult to discern the hidden hands behind some of the incredible bureaucratic decisions that accomplish the wrecking.

How many of us — not excluding this writer — knew in the 1960's of the campaign being carried on against a chemical of nearly miraculous powers, known as DDT? The story of the vicissitudes of dichloro-diphenyl-trichloroethane (DDT) is one of the most remarkable in the annals of chemistry and medicine. It was first synthesized in Germany in 1874 from sulphuric acid, monochlorobenzene, and chloral hydrate, but no use was made of the discovery until 1939, when Paul Mueller, a Swiss scientist, found out that it would kill insects. For this discovery, as its implications astounded the agricultural and medical worlds, Dr. Mueller received the Nobel Prize for physiology in 1948. First tested, with great effect, on Colorado potato beetles in Switzerland, DDT showed its merit in medical practice in 1944, when it wiped out a typhus epidemic in the United States Army in Naples, Italy. Soldiers and civilians there were dusted with the insecticide, newly dispatched from Switzerland. DDT then gained world renown and acceptance. The results of its use were epoch-making.

In Ceylon (now Sri Lanka) ravaged by malaria from time immemorial, DDT reduced the number of cases from millions annually, with 10,000 or more deaths, to only 110 cases in the entire island republic in 1961. In the year following, the book *Silent Spring*, by Rachel Carson, was published and highly publicized by the left-wing news media. It was an eloquent condemnation of pesticides in general and DDT in particular. Not only did the United States goverment respond by taking action against this blessing to mankind, but so did Ceylon. As a result, by 1968 the scourge had returned to Ceylon, with 2,500,000 malaria cases reported, and more than 10,000 deaths. Ceylon soon regained its balance, however, and reinstated DDT, with results identical to those experienced when the chemical was first used. Malaria was again brought under control. The mosquitoes that carry the microscopic malaria parasites apparently were unaware that they were developing great resistance to DDT, as was widely reported by the media.

While bans on the use of DDT in other countries have been lifted, the United States, riding the wave of the future as presented by the controlled press, continues to bar the use of DDT except "on three minor vegetable crops in certain geographic areas under severely restricted conditions." And this is in spite of the fact that a seven months' investigation by the Interior Department in 1972 concluded that there was "a present need for the essential uses of DDT" and that the value of the chemical far outweighed the risks.

The support for DDT on the part of highly qualified professional persons is so extensive that it cannot all be presented here, but some of the testimony presented in *The Disaster Lobby* follows.

Dr. Edward R. Laws, Jr. of The Johns Hopkins University:

It is noteworthy that no cases of cancer developed among these workers [exposed to high levels of DDT for 10 to 20 years] in some 1,300 man-years of exposure, a statistically improbable event.

World Health Organization:

It is obvious that the withdrawal of DDT would indeed be a major tragedy in the chapter of human health. Vast populations of the world would be condemned to the frightening ravages of endemic and epidemic malaria. [It added that tests had proved that DDT was harmless to human beings, even when used as a spray against flies

118

and other pests in homes.]*

Dr. Joseph W. Still, former director of Bucks County (Pa.) Health Department and a former officer in the Army Medical Corps:

There are one *billion* human beings living today healthy who would be either sick or dead without DDT. . . . Although the exaggerated charges [of "so-called environmental protectionists"] have been exposed by competent authorities, these refutations in many cases have not even been mentioned by the mass media which presented the original scare stories. As a result of the anti-DDT hysteria, we are now at the point where politicians may ban the most beneficial chemical known to man because a big publicity campaign has succeeded in giving DDT an image completely false.†

Americans do not suffer from typhus, bubonic plague, cholera, and some of the other diseases that greatly afflict other peoples. Because these diseases are controlled by DDT, this valuable chemical agent will not be abandoned lightly in their countries.

The more one looks at the far-reaching effects of radical environmentalism in the United States, the more apparent it becomes that this movement was designed to keep Americans agitated about the shortcomings of their country — from the no-win war in Vietnam to the "wrongs" committed against other countries, such as Cuba, Chile, and Panama, and to the "terrible" things done to American citizens by the CIA and FBI. "Keep the heat on America" seems to be the watchword; keep the country nervous and bleeding in one way or another.‡

During three years of the first Nixon Administration more than 4.5 billion dollars were spent on ecological projects. And the Environmental Protection Agency was established to police and en-

* The Columbia Broadcasting System on May 11, 1976, presented a TV documentary on the bald eagle in which the narrator spoke of DDT as "a deadly poison." — H.H.D.
†Grayson and Shepard, *op. cit.,* pages 24-39.
‡See *The Rockefeller File,* by Gary Allen.

force Federal environmental standards. The President himself on January 20, 1972, in his State of the Union message, made a highly emotional plea to the Congress. He said:

> [The "environmental awakening" of America] is working a revolution in values, as commitment to responsible partnership with nature replaces cavalier assumptions that we can play God with our surroundings and survive. It is leading to broad reforms in action, as individuals, corporations, government and civic groups mobilize to conserve resources, to control pollution, to anticipate and prevent emerging environmental problems, to manage the land more wisely and preserve wildness.

In the same year, 1972, the Council for Environmental Balance, Inc., was created by scientists concerned lest the "movement" get completely out of hand. Dr. John J. McKetta, professor of chemical engineering at the University of Texas and chairman of the National Air Quality Commission, agreed to serve as vice president of the Council. A talk he gave on the subject of "environmental myths" was printed in *AIM Report,* published by Accuracy In Media, Inc., in November 1974, and in *Human Events* on January 11, 1975, when the "filthy air" hysteria had reached its peak.

The first myth debunked by Dr. McKetta was that the oxygen in our air was being seriously depleted and replaced by noxious gases such as carbon monoxide. He stated that most of the oxygen in our atmosphere came not from plant life but from some other source, most probably from "the photodisassociation of water vapor in the upper atmosphere by high energy rays from the sun and by cosmic rays." He asserted that this method alone could have made "about seven times the present mass of oxygen in the atmosphere," and added that the supply of oxygen was "virtually unlimited" and not threatened "by man's activities in any significant way."

Dr. McKetta then took up the introduction of 270 million tons of carbon monoxide a year into the air by human beings, chiefly produced by automobiles.* He noted that for several years

---

*Carbon monoxide is a highly unstable molecule that will disintegrate in the oper

monitoring stations on land and sea had been checking the carbon monoxide content in the air of both northern and southern hemispheres. Since there are about nine automobiles in the northern hemisphere to every one in the southern, the assumption was that the monitors would find a much higher concentration of the poisonous gas in the north. The measurements, however, showed no difference in the amounts of carbon monoxide in the air in the two hemispheres. And the concentration of the noxious gas in the air was not increasing at all.

Where did the carbon monoxide go? In 1971 scientists at the Stanford Research Institute in California discovered that this gas vanished in smog chambers containing soil in which there were aspergillus fungi. "These organisms, on a world-wide basis," Dr. McKetta said, "are using all of the 270 million tons of CO [carbon monoxide] made by man, for their own metabolism, [and are] thus enriching the soils of the forests and the fields." Carbon monoxide in concentrated amounts is highly poisonous and explosive. But, the Texas professor observed, while carbon monoxide in heavy traffic in downtown Houston may build up to 15 or 20 parts per million (in Los Angeles it reaches 35), the CO content of cigarette smoke is 42,000 parts per million. He concludes, "In the broad expanse of our natural air, CO levels are totally safe for human beings."

Dr. McKetta's commentary hardly fits in with the dire predictions of the doomsday prophets. Accuracy In Media remarked in its introduction to Dr. McKetta's talk:

> The news media have played an important role in alerting the public to environmental problems. However, as is so often the case, the reporting has frequently tended to be one-sided and misleading. There is now a growing recognition that many actions have been taken in this area that have not been based on full consideration of all the facts or which have been grounded in misinformation.

The authors of *The Disaster Lobby* pointed out that "the

---

air. It presents real dangers during its temporary existence when allowed to accumulate in an enclosed space.

stark, unalloyed truth is that the air pollution panic of the 1960's was almost entirely contrived." They cited the assertion of Dr. William T. Pecora, Director of the United States Geological Survey, that "more particulate matter and more combined gases" were hurled into the air by the volcanic eruptions of Krakatoa, in Java, in 1883; Katmai, in Alaska, in 1912, and Hekla, in Iceland, in 1947, "than from all of mankind's activities in recorded history." But, as Professor Thomas Jukes of the University of California said: "Condemning nature is unpopular. The dogma of the environmentalists seems to be that 'only man is vile.' "

The agitated, highly disordered situation in the United States seems made to order for quacks and phonies — as it probably was. Certainly it was no accident that during the violent sixties various corporations, especially the automobile industry, were hit by stringent regulations detailing what they could and could not produce. The motor vehicle companies were required to install seat belts, buzzers, harnesses, and finally anti-pollution devices that ended by causing serious pollution themselves. The monetary cost of all this was fabulous — five billion dollars, more or less, which the consumers paid. But who will ever know what the actual total cost was? Electric utility companies were forbidden to build atomic power-generating plants at certain sites, and in many cases these plants were not built at all. At the same time the companies were of course restricted in their use of coal, and in the early seventies the price of oil skyrocketed, both during and after the Arab oil boycott.

In 1965 a book entitled *Unsafe At Any Speed,* by Ralph Nader, appeared on the American scene. It was embraced with ardor by the leftist news media, to whom it was a trouble-making godsend. Its author was lionized. One would have thought that this unbridled attack upon "the motor vehicle" would have been promptly shot down by the communications media, who should have been interested not only in guarding the people against falsehoods but in protecting one of the vital foundations of the American economy — indeed, of the American way of life. A nearly airtight case against Nader could be made in a book with the title *Safe At Any Reasonable Speed With a Sober Driver.* Nader, in his book, claimed that for "over half a century the automobile has brought death, injury, and the most inestimable sorrow and deprivation to millions of people." Millions? Most doubtful. But the automobile did bring a wholly new life to hundreds of millions who were forced to travel at a snail's pace in the old smelly, fly-ridden horse-and-buggy days.

What did Nader contribute to the safety of human beings, in and out of automobiles? Nothing, according to the authors of *The Disaster Lobby*. Their finding follows:

American automobile manufacturers had been making safer cars year after year before Nader appeared to chastise them. The National Safety Council concluded that the horse-and-carriage was a far more dangerous vehicle, producing ten times as many fatalities per hundred million miles. The Council noted that in 1913 the death rate per 10,000 registered motor vehicles was 23.8. By 1960 the fatalities had reached a record low of 5.1. The Safety Council began totalling auto deaths per 100 million travel miles in 1923. From that year to 1927, the average number of fatalities for every 100 million miles was 18.2, and from 1928 to 1932, 15.6. It fell to 11.4 in 1940, to 7.6 in 1950, and to 5.3 in 1960. This was accomplished despite a tripling in the number of vehicles on the roads since 1939, and in spite of the higher speed achieved. But during the 1960's there was no decline in highway deaths per 100 million miles traveled. This was also the first decade that showed an increase in deaths per 10,000 registered vehicles. In 1972 highway fatalities reached a record total of 57,000.

The newly required safety features average $200 per car, in addition to the cost added to each vehicle for devices that are supposed to reduce exhaust emissions of unwanted gases — the most toxic of which is carbon monoxide. The estimated cost of all this added equipment varies, but the average is $700 per car. And it is all paid for by the consumer, for whom the safety forces profess such tender concern.

Dr. McKetta went on to assert that 93 percent of the carbon monoxide in the atmosphere comes "from trees and greeneries," which contribute 3.5 billion tons a year, as against only 270 million tons a year from man and his automobiles. He also pointed out that air monitors had found higher concentrations of carbon monoxide over the Atlantic and Pacific Oceans than over land. The large cities of the United States, not excluding Los Angeles and New York, reported an improvement in the quality of their air in the decade 1960-70, prior to the use of exhaust safety devices. Moreover, scientific measurement of air around the world showed that the amount of oxygen was the same in 1970 as in 1910.

Although space permits only the briefest mention of this matter, Lake Erie, which was proclaimed to be a "dead lake," in 1972 and 1973 yielded more fish to be sold on the markets than Lake Superior. Indeed, Lake Erie is a piscatorial cornucopia among the Great Lakes — not at all a dead sea as has been claimed. The problem in Lake Erie is pollution from sewage, which uses up oxygen in the lake in the areas adjacent to the large cities of Detroit, Toledo, Sandusky, and Cleveland. The oxidation situation could be corrected by proper sewage treatment. The lake also experiences heat pollution, but the greatest cause of this is the sun, over which man fortunately does not yet exercise control.

More often than not, the environmental movement looks like exactly what it is — a kind of political activism snuggled into the midst of honest efforts to protect the fauna and flora, the permafrost and the wooded hills of the country. Such was the case when oil was discovered on the North Slope of Alaska in the 1960's. It brought the prospect of an additional two million barrels a day of badly needed petroleum for domestic consumption, but even though American oil companies were eager to bring this oil to market regardless of the enormous cost for doing so (naturally, in the hope of recouping their vast outlays for discovery and pipeline construction), the protectors of flowers and caribou were able to put off the construction of the Alaska Pipeline for more than four years — in spite of the fact that the pipe had already been shipped to Alaska. If it is true that this is how the pipeline was delayed, then we must accept the idea that relatively very few environmentalists, largely unknown to the public, were able to exercise more influence over the government than the general public (especially the people of Alaska) and the not entirely impotent oil companies. The gnomes of New York do not believe that. They saw the matter of the Alaska Pipeline as a power struggle involving titanic forces, among whom the environmentalists were the least considerable of all. But the term ecology sparkled all over the place during the contest.*

Some vital statistics and other facts pertinent to this controversy follow:

The United States used about 15 million barrels of oil a day in 1970, of which it produced less than 10 million barrels, as the construction of the pipeline was being held up. By 1975 domestic consumption was at 17.5 million barrels. And it was predicted as far back as 1973 that the country would need 20 million barrels per day by 1980. The Alaska wells will yield about 2 million barrels each day. Massive imports of oil will continue to be necessary unless new petroleum is found or released and additional energy is produced by nuclear, solar, wind, tidal, and oceanic thermal means. The United States is too large an exporter to be absolutely self-sufficient. But it cannot allow its economy (and politics) to be interfered with deliberately by a country (or a cartel) that quadruples its oil prices on an *or else* basis.

The ability of various environmentalist forces to halt energy production or energy conservation has been shown in other areas. Some projects that have been halted or are under attack are listed here: Cross-Florida Barge Canal; Gila River Channelizing, Arizona; New Hope Reservoir, North Carolina; West Tennessee Tributaries; Cache River Flood Control, Arkansas; Gillham Dam, Arkansas; La Farge Reservoir, Wisconsin; Oakley Reservoir, Illinois; Cooper Lake and Channels Project, Texas; Laneport Dam, Texas; Wallisville Dam, Texas; Lower Granite and Asotin Dam, Washington; East Fork Lake, Ohio. In 1976 the $3.5 billion Kaparowits electric power project in Utah was killed outright.

Dr. Petr Beckmann, a distinguished scientist who left Czechoslovakia to become a professor of electrical engineering at the University of Colorado, wrote in *The Review Of The News* on

---

* At first the ecologists asserted that the pipeline would threaten the existence of the Alaskan caribou. After tests proved that the caribou would coexist happily with the pipeline, the environmentalists shifted ground and cried that the pipeline would cause Alaska to be overrun by caribou.

125

July 23, 1975, that "even the environmentalist groups seem moderate compared with such movements as the one launched last November by Ralph Nader at the 'Critical Mass '74' rally." Dr. Beckmann said it had "strong totalitarian overtones" and that it flatly ignored "all technological considerations in favor of purely political notions." Indeed, Nader himself had claimed that the meeting presaged "the beginning of a democratic control of all technology." And that assertion undoubtedly indicates the actual goal of most environmentalist actions, unknown, of course, to most environmentalists. Dr. Beckmann pointed out:

The three television networks give exaggerated coverage to Nader's hysteria, but last February they censored a unique appeal for nuclear power by 34 of this country's foremost scientists, including 11 Nobel Prize winners. Their "documentaries" on nuclear power attempt to give the impression of fairness by balancing the truth against a lie, giving them equal weight, and even then they smuggle in the savage distortions of the half-truth. They endlessly exploit the psychological association of *nuclear* and *bomb*, which makes as much sense as the association of *electric* and *chair*.

The national newspapers and weeklies are hardly better, and the distortions are by no means limited to what is thought of as the "Liberal" press. The *Wall Street Journal*, for instance, has many times fallen for Nader's hoaxes on the unreliability of nuclear plants and alleged accidents, and has not published corrections when the dishonesty of these reports was pointed out to its editors. *Business Week* has gone so far as to editorialize on the "Faustian Bargain Of Nuclear Power" and similar melodramatic piffle.

Dr. Beckmann observed that in spite of the fact that "Ralph Nader has become the laughing stock of the nuclear industry," the public and public officials had sincere doubts about the safety of nuclear power plants, that some States had restricted the building of such plants, and that Californians would vote in 1976 on a referendum that posed the question whether the State should virtually halt nuclear power. After explaining how atomic power makes electricity by generating the heat to produce steam for turbogenerators, this distinguished scientist discussed the ultimate point that the public wants answered, thus:

It is physically impossible to induce an explosive nuclear chain reaction in the uranium used for fuel in power plants. Anti-nuclear horror stories, such as Nader's fable of "100,000 deaths and the destruction of an area the size of Pennsylvania" are undiluted hogwash. A nuclear explosion in a power plant is not merely improbable, it is impossible: An explosive chain reaction is no more feasible in 3 per cent enriched uranium than it is in chewing gum.

Dr. Beckmann pointed out that 1,060 miners lose their lives in producing the coal required to produce 1 billion kilowatt hours of electricity — 1,000 from black lung, and 60 in accidents. He asserted that only 20 lives are lost among the miners who dig out the uranium to produce that amount of electricity. And he stated that the use of breeder reactors to produce electricity would reduce the loss of life among uranium miners to .07 per 1 billion kilowatt hours of electricity.

The twentieth century opposition to nuclear power plants may one day be considered comparable to the attacks upon machines by craftsmen and peasants in the previous century.

When a major error is made in the news, the correction, if there is one, rarely catches up with the mistake. After so many years of observation, I no longer find it strange that the national news media are in no haste to correct errors, especially those which they have disseminated. A number of the matters dealt with in this chapter are exemplary of this point. Since this writer, himself a student of the news, was surprised when he learned the truth about some of these myths, he was not astonished to find that many other persons, some highly knowledgeable, knew as little of the truth as he did.

Unfortunately, much more is being done in the name of ecology or pursuant to governmental programs than can even be mentioned in this chapter. And those subjects that we have covered have not been dealt with exhaustively. We have merely introduced the reader to this field in an attempt to show how some of the bleeding of America has been accomplished. Again, those who desire more information are urged to consult the sources cited in the bibliography for the details that are lacking here.

On October 19, 1975, the Manion Forum radio program consisted of an interview with Dr. John J. McKetta, the chemical engineering professor whom we quoted earlier concerning air pollution. Some of Dr. McKetta's remarks on the energy crisis are so compellingly apropos that we quote them here.

> Sometimes it seems that this country's politicians, environmentalists and conservationists are linked together into a plot to bring America to eventual disaster by making domestic energy expansion impossible. Most sensible people know that the problems of higher taxes, price controls, threat of excess profit penalties, embargoes on leasing or operating in favorable coastal areas, and rigid excessive environmental requirements serve only as roadblocks in efforts to explore for new reserves or to build new facilities. . . .
>
> The American Electric Power Company . . . built the huge John Amos Coal Plant on a large coal field near Charleston, West Virginia. This is the largest coal burning electrical plant in the world. After the plant was built, EPA [the Environmental Protection Agency] required that low sulfur coal be used rather than the West Virginia coal at that plant. Now coal is being delivered from the Western United States to St. Louis overland, and then by barge to Charleston, West Virginia. At the same time these coal barges are going up the Ohio River, they pass coal barges coming from West Virginia hauling coal down the Ohio River. This latter coal is being sold to Western States and to Germany and Japan.
>
> Incidentally, the fuel used for all of this coal delivery is oil — which, as every one knows, is much scarcer than coal.

Dr. McKetta maintained that, to cope with the energy crisis, we should declare a moratorium on many things. As examples he listed the following:

> Disposable containers. Air conditioning in automobiles. Catalytic converters on tail pipes and all exhaust gas recirculation in automobiles (except in Los Angeles and the few cities that have the chimney effect in the downtown areas). We must put an end to the production of large cars by 1980. We must build no more buildings that can't have their windows opened. We have to put lead back into

gasoline. We must retain the 55 mph speed laws and we must increase mass transportation many-fold.

Dr. McKetta condemned the "inept inactivity of the U.S. Congress" in dealing with the energy crisis as conduct that "borders on treason."

CHAPTER 10

Pearl Harbor: "A Date Which Will Live In Infamy"

There is excuse for defeat, but none for surprise.
— Military maxim

THIS BOOK WOULD NOT BE complete without mention of the attack on Pearl Harbor on December 7, 1941. Indeed, this tragic and unnecessary event was precipitated by our own government in order to give Franklin Roosevelt the justification he needed to bring America into World War II. And this premeditated treachery led to the sacrifice of 3,077 lives of Navy and Marine Corps men, with 876 wounded, and 226 lives of Army and Army Air Corps men, with 396 wounded. The Japanese were deliberately drawn in to make the attack — drawn in by President Roosevelt, who afterward declared sanctimoniously that December 7, 1941, was a "date which will live in infamy."

The idea that a President of the United States would be guilty of such treachery was so revolting and repugnant to this writer that he scornfully rejected it when it was first posed to him in New York in December of 1941. Naïveté? Yes, there was some of that. But in extenuation of his unwillingness to believe the worst about a President of the United States, the writer offers this much in explanation:

He was then an assistant foreign editor of *The New York Times*, a position in which he was required to read daily virtually all the foreign news that came in to that newspaper — the *Times's* own voluminous file of its correspondents around the world, the Associated Press, United Press, Reuters, Jewish News Agency, Religious News Agency, and a scattering of other contributions, if his eyes were still holding up at the end of the evening.

With his knowledge of current foreign affairs, the writer was able to predict on the night before Pearl Harbor — December 6, 1941 — that the United States would be at war with Japan before the month was out. This prediction was based upon a dispatch from Otto D. Tolischus in Tokyo to the *New York Times* on December 6. The substance of the Tolischus article was read over WQXR, the *Times'* radio station, that evening. It was that the Government of Japan had issued a statement to the Japanese people that, *if war should come,* they should feel confident that Japan was capable of fighting to victory. The statement then listed the number of planes and warships possessed by Japan and provided other particulars concerning Japanese fighting strength.

The writer realized that every government, without exception, prepares its people for great operations such as war. And he observed that the *Times* dispatch clearly showed that Japan was preparing its people for war with the United States, and that the outbreak of that war would occur during the month of December. This did not seem especially clairvoyant at the moment, though the fulfillment of the prophecy the very next day was stunning.

Now he felt that his sources of information, while extraordinarily large and timely, were no better than those of the United States Government (and, of course, they were not). Therefore, it seemed to him to have been just plain malfeasance on the part of the commanders at Pearl Harbor not to have been prepared and waiting for the Japanese. But those commanders — Admiral Husband E. Kimmel of the United States Navy and General Walter C. Short of the United States Army — depended upon their superiors in Washington to keep them advised, as they had every right to do.

There is now a wealth of evidence — conclusive evidence — that the Japanese were enticed into making the attack which led to so great a loss of American lives and fighting capability. Eight battleships were knocked out of action, along with three cruisers. Four destroyers were damaged (two beyond repair). A seaplane tender and a repair ship were badly damaged; a target ship was sunk; one hundred seventy-seven American planes were destroyed on the ground. The Japanese lost 48 planes and three midget submarines.

131

But let us not forget that the Japanese were lured into the attack on Pearl Harbor, while the American commanders there were kept in ignorance of impending onslaught. This fact is now established beyond question. But the public as a whole unfortunately still is generally ignorant of these facts.

Dr. Anthony C. Kubek, mentioned earlier herein as the author of *How The Far East Was Lost*, wrote in that work, on page 18:

> At noon on November 25 [1941], Secretaries [Henry L.] Stimson [War] and [Frank] Knox [Navy] met at the White House together with General [George C.] Marshall [Army Chief of Staff] and Admiral [Harold R.] Stark [Chief of Naval Operations]. The discussion dealt mainly with the Japanese situation concerning the intercepted message fixing the November 29 deadline. [A secret Japanese deadline which the United States — that is, Washington — learned about by intercepting a Tokyo message to its embassy in Washington. The United States had broken the Japanese code.] The President brought up the event that we were likely to be attacked perhaps (as soon as) next Monday, for the Japanese are notorious for making an attack without warning. The main question was how we should maneuver them into the position of firing the first shot without allowing too much danger to ourselves. It was a difficult proposition.

The difficulty, of course, was overcome, and the Japanese were permitted to make their attack without even being discovered by American planes. There was no message of warning from General Marshall to General Short, or from Admiral Stark to Admiral Kimmel, in time to meet the attack. General Marshall offered this incredible explanation for the failure:

> That morning [Dec. 7, 1941] in Washington, General Marshall had sent a message to General Short in Honolulu, instructing him to be on the alert. Marshall did not use the scrambler telephone that would have put him in direct touch with General Short. Instead, he sent the warning by commercial cable [!], and it arrived too late [hours after the attack]. Explaining his activities of that morning, Marshall said that he did not use the telephone because the Japanese might take the alerting of American garrisons in Hawaii as a hostile

act [!]. He said, "The Japanese would have grasped at almost any straw to bring to such portions of our public that doubted our integrity of action that we were committing an act that forced action on their part." In other words, Marshall was saying, never mind about American men who may be killed by surprise without a chance to fight, so long as we don't lay ourselves open to criticism by isolationists. Marshall's statement made little sense, for he *had* alerted Short, but by a roundabout method that turned out to be ineffectual under the pressure of events. After sending the telegram, Marshall went out for a [horseback] ride in Rock Creek Park.*

The Japanese already were en route to attack Pearl Harbor, certainly without worrying about whether or not we would accuse them of provocation. Their action had undoubtedly been prepared many days in advance. Marshall's explanation of this affair makes as little sense as some of the reasons given for his other moves as a statesman, which were so often disastrous. Coincidentally but revealingly, Admiral Stark also refused to notify Admiral Kimmel.

The method by which the United States decoded the all- important messages between Tokyo and the Japanese Embassy in Washington was called Magic. The messages showed the great interest of the Japanese in the positions of United States warships in Pearl Harbor, and they certainly foretold the beginning of the war. Rear Admiral Robert A. Theobald, U.S.N., ret., was Commander, Destroyers, Battle Force, and was in Pearl Harbor when the Japanese struck. He wrote a book, *The Final Secret of Pearl Harbor,* published in 1954 by Devin-Adair, which is the definitive statement on the attack for Navy men. It is a moving one, too, with corroborative forewords by Admiral Kimmel and Fleet Admiral William F. Halsey. Admiral Halsey's position is succinctly stated in his final paragraph:

> I have always considered Admiral Kimmel and General Short to be splendid officers who were thrown to the wolves as scapegoats for something over which they had no control. They had to work with what they were given, both in equipment and information. They are our outstanding military martyrs.

FDR, by Finis Farr, page 373.

133

Admiral Halsey pinpoints the situation in this paragraph:

> At that time [the day of the attack] I was one of the three senior commanders of the Pacific Fleet, serving under Admiral Kimmel. I am sure he kept me informed of all the intelligence he possessed. Certainly I did not know then of any of the pertinent Magic Messages. All our intelligence pointed to an attack by Japan against the Philippines or the southern areas in Malaya or the Dutch East Indies. While Pearl Harbor was considered and not ruled out, the mass of the evidence made available to us pointed in another direction. Had we known of Japan's minute and continued interest in the exact location and movement of our ships in Pearl Harbor, as indicated in the Magic Messages, it is only logical that we would have concentrated our thought on meeting the practical certainty of an attack on Pearl Harbor.

Admiral Halsey advised "every American who believes in fair play" to read Admiral Theobald's book. That is an excellent suggestion to all who are interested in what really happened at Pearl Harbor. Meanwhile, read these paragraphs from the book:

> Everything that happened in Washington on Saturday and Sunday, December 6 and 7, supports the belief that President Roosevelt had directed that no message be sent to Hawaiian Commanders before noon on Sunday, Washington time.
>
> General Marshall apparently appreciated that failure to act on the Declaration of War message [by Japan on Dec. 6] and its timed delivery [to the United States on Dec. 7] was going to be very difficult to explain on the witness stand when the future inevitable investigation into the incidents of those days took place. His avoidance of contact with the messages after the Pilot message until 11:25 on Sunday morning [December 7] was unquestionably prompted by these thoughts. Otherwise, he would undoubtedly have been in his office at 8 A.M. on that fateful day.
>
> Admiral Stark, on the other hand, did arrive in his office at 9:25 A.M. on Sunday, and at once accepted delivery of the full [Japanese] Declaration of War message. Against the advice of his assistants, he refused to inform Admiral Kimmel of its receipt. Forty minutes later, he knew that the 14-part message was to be delivered

to the U.S. Government at 1:00 P.M., Washington time, which was 7:30 A.M., Hawaiian time, as was pointed out to him at once. Again, despite the urging of certain of his aides, he refused to send word to Admiral Kimmel.

Never before in recorded history had a field commander been denied information that his country would be at war in a matter of hours, and that everything pointed to a surprise attack upon his forces shortly after sunrise. No Naval officer, on his own initiative, would ever make such a decision as Admiral Stark thus did.

That fact, and Admiral Stark's decisions on that Sunday morning, even if they had not been supported by the wealth of earlier evidence, would reveal, beyond question, the basic truth of the Pearl Harbor story, namely that these Sunday messages and so many earlier ones, of vital import to Admiral Kimmel's exercise of his command, were not sent because Admiral Stark had orders form the President, which prohibited that action.

This deduction is fully supported by the Admiral's statement to the press in August, 1945, that all he did during the pre-Pearl Harbor days was done on order of higher authority, which can only mean President Roosevelt. The most arresting thing he did, during that time, was to withhold information from Admiral Kimmel.

Thus, by holding a weak Pacific Fleet in Hawaii as an invitation to a surprise attack, and by denying the Commander of that fleet the information which might cause him to render that attack impossible, President Roosevelt brought war to the United States on December 7, 1941. He took a fully aroused nation into the fight because none of its people suspected how the Japanese surprise attack fitted into their President's plans.

That last sentence is misleading on two counts. Some Americans did suspect how the Japanese attack fitted into President Roosevelt's plans and said so in the most vigorous language to his writer. Also, the nation was well aroused, and could have been taken into the war without the unnecessary sacrifice of men, ships, and planes. December 7, 1941, is indeed "a date which will live in infamy."

Epilogue

MANY PHASES OF THE bleeding of America have not been touched upon in this work. The interaction between the United States and other nations will immediately come to mind. How much has the holding back of the United States and the building up of the Soviet Union interfered with normal relations between the United States and its allies around the world? No one will ever know. But the matter is not entirely beyond the range of study. Some Europeans by 1970 were calling the United States "the muscle-bound giant," and one European leader sneered that the United States was not politically capable of leading the world.

The Laocoön posture of the United States *invited* attacks by its enemies, so that with the increasing loss of blood and strength, and the never-ending refusal to stand up for its rights in the world, America became a forbidding figure to its friends. For our allies and potential allies, it became a matter of *sauve qui peut,* while the country that had led the world to victory against the greatest threat ever posed by a totalitarian nation found itself being shorn of its strength; at the same time it was urged to give succor to every nation that asked for it.

This work has only touched the subject of massive news distortion, omission, and fabrication by the media of communication. Their aim, practically speaking, has been to make the Soviet and

Chinese Communists look different from what they are — either stronger or weaker to suit the particular need of the moment. The great misdeeds of the Russian Communists in their subjugated lands, especially in Eastern Europe, have been almost entirely ignored by the press, or painted in bright colors. A new ethic has evolved. It approves any kind of inhumanity to mankind so long as we can stay on our knees and do nothing to give our Communist enemies, at home and abroad, the slightest impression that we will ever refuse to yield to any of their demands that the American public can be made to swallow. This is an area that desperately needs study by the American people.

The weakening of the United States in relation to the Soviet Union has brought a train of security abuses with it. The abuses have taken many forms, some of which have been described in this work. But there was insufficient space to discuss numerous others, though many of them will be apparent to the reader. Once a fundamental bleeding of America was started, stanching of the wound became as impossible as it was unwanted by those who had inflicted it. The rejection of security in the State Department was indicated. The loss of Cuba to Communism was a foregone "happening." The great inflationary grain sale to the Russians in 1972 was inevitable. The attempt to turn the minds of the people to riotous sex and drugs (marijuana and heroin) was predictably certain. A grave weakening of the nation's currency became an obvious purpose. The one desperate fear of our esoteric policy-makers is that the United States might again become overwhelmingly strong and orderly.

The balance of power, tilted against the United States abroad, was equally loaded against it at home. The giveaway programs pushed by the Communists and other radicals as roads to inflation and chaos were put into effect by those who intended to maintain the balance. Since any number could play the game, the use of the wildly proliferating greenbacks was fun for most of the people, at first. But when the inevitable devaluation and depreciation of the currency became devastating at home and abroad, the game was no longer amusing.

There are, indeed, phases of the bleeding, both internally and externally, that must be investigated. It is perhaps too early to ask scholars in our universities to undertake this work, since they are more often concerned with the past than with contemporary historical events. Others can and should pitch in and do the job. Some phases of the ecological movement are deserving of study. For instance, why was the Alaska oil pipeline delayed for more than four years on the specious grounds that certain fauna and flora might be unfavorably affected? Precisely why was Cuba handed over to the Communists? Why did the United States do nothing to prevent the Communist move to take over Portugal? What role or roles does the Communist Party play in the United States? To what extent is pornography deliberately designed to bleed America? This is a large, unworked field. This writer claims only to have begun some preliminary digging. The larger stories still lie buried beneath a mound of silence.

BIBLIOGRAPHY

"AAAS: Hard Science or Soft Issues." *Science News*, February 8, 1975, pp. 86-87.

Gary Allen. *None Dare Call It Conspiracy*. Rossmoor, California: Concord Press, 1972.

——. *The Rockefeller File*. Seal Beach, California: '76 Press, 1976.

Bernadine Bailey. *The Captive Nations*. Chicago: Charles Halberg and Company, 1969.

James Bales. *The Phoenix Papers*. Tulsa, Oklahoma: Christian Crusade, 1966.

Petr Beckmann. "Reactors and Radical Reaction." *The Review Of The News*, July 23, 1975

Arnold Beichman. *The Nine Lies About America*. Library Press, 1972.

Paul D. Bethel. *The Losers*. New Rochelle, New York: Arlington House, 1969.

Otto L. Bettmann. *The Good Old Days — They Were Terrible!* New York: Random House, 1975.

Charles E. Bohlen. *Witness to History*. New York: W.W. Norton, 1973.

Spruille Braden. *Diplomats and Demagogues: The Memoirs of Spruille Braden*. New Rochelle, New York: Arlington House, 1971.

James F. Byrnes. *Speaking Frankly*. New York: Harper, 1947.

Ronald W. Clark. *Einstein: The Life and Times*. New York, Cleveland: World Publishing, 1971.

Phoebe Courtney. *The CFR: America's Unelected Rulers*. New Orleans: Free Men Speak, Inc., 1968.

Curtis B. Dall. *F.D.R.: My Exploited Father-In-Law*. Washington, D.C.: Liberty Lobby, 1970.

Ralph de Toledano. *Hit and Run: The Rise — And Fall? — of Ralph Nader*. New Rochelle, New York: Arlington House, 1975.

James Dines. *The Invisible Crash*. New York: Random House, 1975.

BIBLIOGRAPHY

Milovan Djilas. *Conversations with Stalin.* New York: Harcourt, Brace and Company, 1962.

John Dornberg. *The New Tsars.* Garden City, New York: Doubleday, 1972.

Hilaire du Berrier. *Background to Betrayal: The Tragedy of Vietnam.* Belmont , Massachusetts: Western Islands, 1965.

Will and Ariel Durant. *The Lessons of History.* New York: Simon and Schuster, 1968.

Miles P. DuVal, Jr. *And The Mountains Will Move.* Westport, Connecticut: Greenwood Press, 1940.

——. *Cadiz to Cathay.* Westport, Connecticut: Greenwood Press, 1940.

Medford Evans. "The Second Atomic Age." *The Review Of The News,* August 6, 1975.

——. *The Secret War for the A-Bomb.* Chicago: Henry Regnery Company, 1953.

M. Stanton Evans. "General Patton in Detroit." *Human Events.* December 21, 1974.

Finis Farr. *FDR.* New Rochelle, New York: Arlington House 1972.

John T. Flynn. *The Lattimore Story.* Old Greenwich, Connecticut Devin-Adair, 1953.

——. *While You Slept.* Old Greenwich, Connecticut: Devin-Adair 1951.

Seymour Freidin and George Bailey. *The Experts.* New York: Macmillan, 1968.

J.W.Fulbright. *The Arrogance of Power.* New York: Random House, 1966.

Martin Gershen. *Destroy or Die.* New Rochelle, New York Arlington House, 1971.

Martin Gilbert. *Russian History Atlas.* New York: Macmillan 1972.

William J. Gill. *The Ordeal of Otto Otepka.* New Rochelle, New York: Arlington House, 1969.

Melvin J. Grayson and Thomas R Shepard, Jr. *The Disaster Lobby* Chicago: Follett Publishing Company, 1973.

G. Edward Griffin. *The Fearful Master.* Belmont, Massachusetts Western Islands, 1964.

Stanley Hoffman, editor. *Conditions of World Order*. Boston: Houghton Mifflin Company, 1966.

Pierre Huss and George Carpozi, Jr. *Red Spies in The U.N.* New York: Coward-McCann, 1965.

J. Bernard Hutton. *The Subverters.* New Rochelle, New York: Arlington House, 1972.

Peter J. Huxley-Blythe. *The East Came West.* Caldwell, Idaho: Caxton Printers, 1968.

Peter N. James. *Soviet Conquest from Space*. New Rochelle, New York: Arlington House, 1974.

George Racey Jordan. *From Major Jordan's Diaries*. Belmont, Massachusetts: Western Islands, 1965.

H.S. Kenan. *The Federal Reserve Bank*. Los Angeles: Noontide Press, 1968.

Jeane J. Kirkpatrick, editor. *The Strategy of Deception: A Study in World-Wide Communist Tactics*. New York: Farrar, Straus and Company, 1963.

Arthur Krock. *Memoirs*. New York: Funk and Wagnalls, 1968.

——. *The Consent of the Governed*. Boston: Little, Brown, and Company, 1971.

Anthony C. Kubek. *How the Far East Was Lost*. Chicago: Henry Regnery Company, 1963.

Suzanne Labin. *Hippies, Drugs and Promiscuity*. New Rochelle, New York: Arlington House, 1972.

Suzanne Labin and Daniel Lyons. *Fifty Years: USSR vs. USA*. New York: Twin Circle, 1968.

Arthur Bliss Lane. *I Saw Poland Betrayed*. Indianapolis: Bobbs-Merrill, 1948.

Thomas A. Lane. *America On Trial*. New Rochelle, New York: Arlington House, 1972.

——. *The War for the World*. San Diego, California: Viewpoint Books, 1968.

Mario Lazo. *Dagger in the Heart: American Policy Failures in Cuba*. New York: Twin Circle, 1970.

Isaac Don Levine. *Eyewitness to History*. New York: Hawthorn Books, 1973.

Dean Manion and Louis C. Wyman. *Freedom of Choice*. South Bend, Indiana: Manion Forum, September 8, 1974.

BIBLIOGRAPHY

Herbert Marcuse. *Essay on Liberation.* Boston: Beacon Press, 1969.
———. *Five Lectures.* Boston: Beacon Press, 1970.
W.S. McBirnie. *How Safe Are You?* Glendale, California: Community Churches of America, 1975.
Joseph R. McCarthy. *America's Retreat From Victory.* Old Greenwich, Connecticut: Devin-Adair, 1951.
Eugene H. Methvin. *The Riot Makers.* New Rochelle, New York: Arlington House, 1970.
Drew Middleton. *Retreat from Victory.* New York: Hawthorn Books, 1973.
Leonard Mosley. *On Borrowed Time.* New York: Random House, 1969.
Gerhart Niemeyer. *Deceitful Peace.* New Rochelle, New York: Arlington House, 1971.
Stephen Pan and Raymond J. De Jaegher. *Peking's Red Guards.* New York: Twin Circle, 1968.
Stephen Pan and Daniel Lyons. *Vietnam Crisis.* New York: Twin Circle, 1966.
R. Hart Phillips. *The Cuban Dilemma.* Obolensky, 1962.
Charles A. Reich. *The Greening of America.* New York: Random House, 1970.
Nelson A. Rockefeller. *The Future of Federalism.* Cambridge: Harvard University Press, 1962.
Phyllis Schlafly and Chester Ward. *Kissinger on the Couch.* New Rochelle, New York: Arlington House, 1975.
Philippa Schuyler. *Good Men Die.* New York: Twin Circle, 1969.
Paul Seabury, editor. *Balance of Power.* San Francisco: Chandler Publishing, 1965.
Elaine Shepard. *Forgive Us Our Press Passes.* Englewood Cliffs, New Jersey: Prentice-Hall, 1962.
———. *The Doom Pussy.* New York: Trident Press, 1962.
Anatol Shub. *The New Russian Tragedy.* New York: W.W. Norton and Company, 1969.
W. Cleon Skousen. *The Naked Capitalist.* Salt Lake City, Utah, 1970.
Jon P. Speller. *The Panama Canal.* New York: Speller and Sons, 1972.

BIBLIOGRAPHY

Nicholas J. Spykman. *America's Strategy in World Politics: The United States and the Balance of Power*. New York: Harcourt, Brace and Company, 1942.

Antony Sutton. *National Suicide*. New Rochelle, New York: Arlington House, 1973.

——. *Wall Street and the Bolshevik Revolution*. New Rochelle, New York: Arlington House, 1974.

——. *Western Technology and Soviet Economic Development* (Three volumes). Stanford: Hoover Institution Press, 1968, 1970, 1973.

Robert A. Theobald. *The Final Secret of Pearl Harbor*. Old Greenwich, Connecticut: Devin-Adair, 1954.

Harry S Truman. *Memoirs*. Garden City, New York: Doubleday, 1956.

Eliseo Vivas. *Contra Marcuse*. New Rochelle, New York: Arlington House, 1971.

Robert Welch. *The Politician*. Belmont, Massachusetts: Belmont Publishing Company, 1964.

Alice Widener. *Behind the U.N. Front*. New York: Bookmailer, 1955.

BIBLIOGRAPHY

INDEX

Abzug, Bella. 100
Accuracy In Media, 8n.-9n., 87, 120, 121
Acheson, Dean, 30, 31, 38, 88, 104
Acheson-Lilienthal Report (*A Report on the International Control of Atomic Energy*), 38, 40
Adriatic Sea, 10
Aetna Standard, 57
Afghanistan, 94
AFL-CIO, 62
Alamogordo, (N.M.), 3
Alaska, 17, 124
Alaskan Pipeline, 124-25, 138
Albania, 34, 101
Aldanov, Mark, 72
Aldenzoloto, 49
Allen, Gary, 46, 74,110, 119n.
All The News That Fits, vi, vii
Altai Mountains, 49
America and Russia in a Changing World, 1n.
American Electric Power Company, 128
American Nuclear Society, 43
America's Retreat from Victory, 27, 71
America's Strategy in World Politics: The United States and the Balance of Power, 16n.
Anderson, Jack, 90
Anderson, Robert B., 106
An-loc (S. Vietnam), 59, 61
Ardahan (Turkey), 34
Argentina, 103
Argonne Laboratory, 20, 41
Arizona Republic, 18, 64
Army and Navy Club (Washington, D.C.), 2
Arthur J. Brandt Company, 59
Ashbrook, Representative John M., 55
Associated Press, 7, 100, 130
Atlantic Charter, 10
Atomic bomb, 2, 3, 4
Atomic materials, 1, 4, 6, 11, 19, 37, 42, 43, 44

Atomic Development Authority, 38-39, 40
Austin Company, 58
Avars, 35

Bacher, Dr. Robert F., 41-43
Bagge, Carl E., 114, 116
Bailey, George, 100, 101
Ball, George W., 79
Baltimore Sun, 8n., 9n.
Banks, Arthur, 35
Baruch, Bernard, 31, 38
Batista, Fulgencio, 109
Bay of Pigs, 109
Beckmann, Petr, 112, 125, 126, 127
Bernhard, Prince of the Netherlands, 24
Berrigans, 90
Berryman, Paul R., 21
Bethel, Paul D., 108, 109
Bevin, Ernest, 67
Biafra, 77
Bilderbergers, 10, 14, 24
Black Liberation Movement, 75
Blair, Harrison D., 21
Bleeding of America, The, vii, viii
Bohlen, Charles E., 4, 5
Bolivia, 93
Borlaug, Norman, 112
Boston, 2, 29, 44
Boudin, Leonard, 90
Bradbury, Dr. Norris E., 42
Braden, Spruille, 101-104
Brady, N.C., 50n.
Brandt, Willy, 104n.
Brennan, Donald, 81
Brezhnev Doctrine, 34-35
Brezhnev, Leonid I., 22, 23, 26, 53, 86n.
Britain, 1, 3, 7, 32, 36, 37, 51, 55, 56, 67, 68, 110
Brown, H. Rap, 95
Buenos Aires, 103
Bulgaria (Bulgarians), 10, 34, 54, 71, 72
Bunker, Ellsworth, 107

145

INDEX

Index

The Bleeding
Of America

The truth is, to be sure, sometimes hard to grasp, but it is never so elusive as when it is not wanted.

— **Herman H. Dinsmore**

Why, it is being asked, should the most powerful country in the world, after an unbroken record of success, descend with such devastating swiftness from its position of towering pre-eminence into the depths in which it is floundering today? That inspired analyst, Mr. Herman H. Dinsmore, a former editor of the *New York Times* International Edition, provides a number of answers. These go quite a long way towards explaining the extraordinary and disconcerting phenomenon which is causing the Western world such disquiet today.

Mr. Dinsmore is much to be complimented in having provided a most significant work . . . . What he has said with such force and clarity is far too true to be good.

A.H. Stanton Candlin
East-West Digest

About the Author

Herman Dinsmore, born in Baltimore and educated at The Johns Hopkins University, was editor of the International Edition of the *New York Times* from 1951 to 1960. He had served on its foreign desk since 1929. He has taught journalism at the Columbia University Graduate School of Journalism, and at Long Island and Seton Hall Universities. Author of a previous book, *All The News That Fits*, Mr. Dinsmore brings a lifetime of experience in journalism to bear in his analysis of the bleeding of America.

$3.00